The Victorian Dining Room

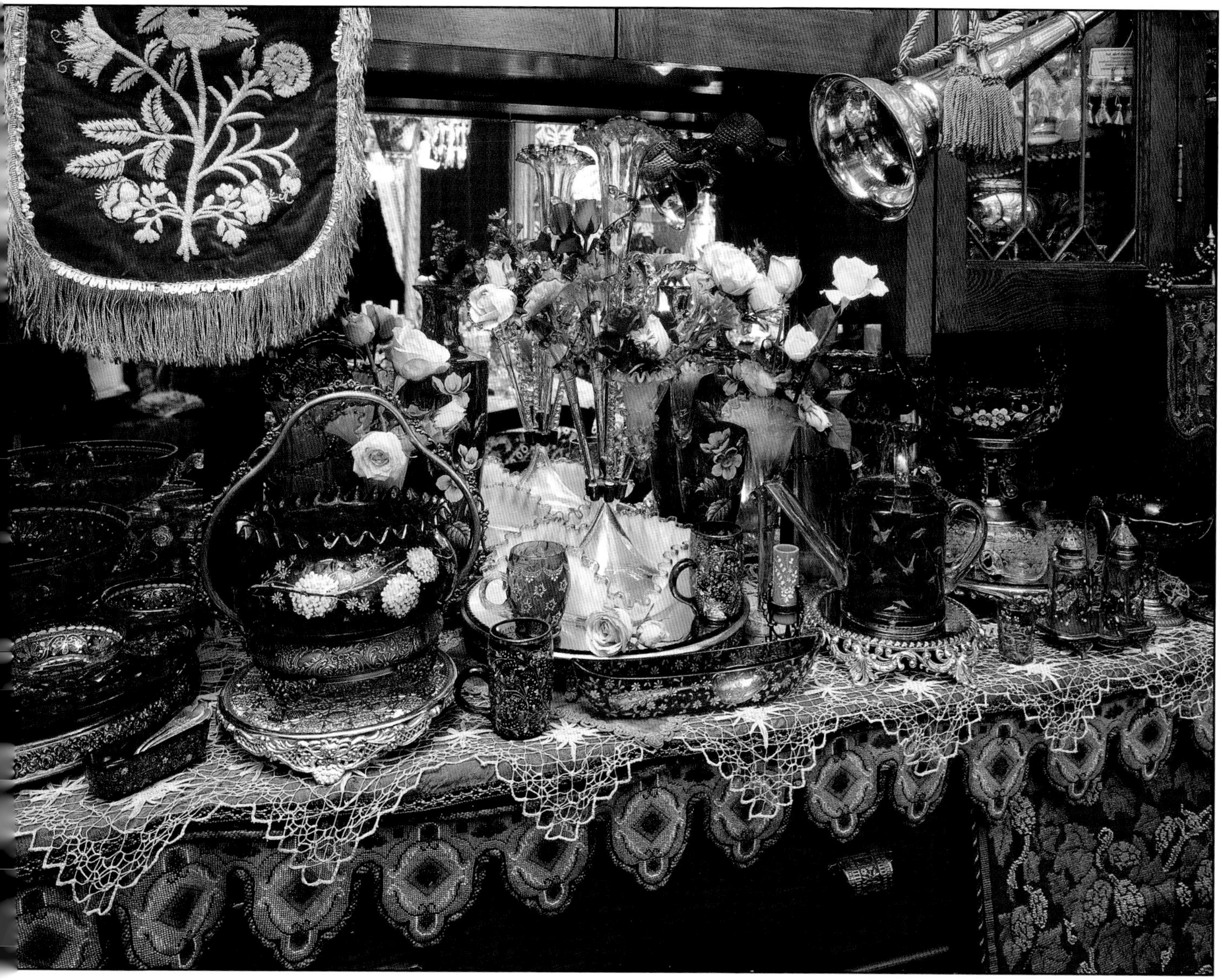

Brian D. Coleman

Principle Photographer, Linda Svendsen

4880 Lower Valley Road, Atglen, PA 19310 USA

Library of Congress Control Number: 2002117605

Designed by Bonnie M. Hensley
Cover designed by Bruce Waters
Type set in Shelley Allegro BT/Dutch 801 BT

ISBN: 0-7643-1792-X
Printed in China
1 2 3 4

Published by Schiffer Publishing Ltd.
4880 Lower Valley Road
Atglen, PA 19310
Phone: (610) 593-1777; Fax: (610) 593-2002
E-mail: Schifferbk@aol.com
Please visit our web site catalog at **www.schifferbooks.com**
We are always looking for people to write books on new and related subjects. If you have an idea for a book please contact us at the above address.

This book may be purchased from the publisher. Include $3.95 for shipping.
Please try your bookstore first. You may write for a free catalog.

In Europe, Schiffer books are distributed by
Bushwood Books
6 Marksbury Ave.
Kew Gardens
Surrey TW9 4JF England
Phone: 44 (0) 20 8392-8585; Fax: 44 (0) 20 8392-9876
E-mail: Bushwd@aol.com
Free postage in the U.K., Europe; air mail at cost.

Dedication

This book is dedicated to my parents, Merri Lynn and Sidney Coleman.

Acknowledgment

Special thanks are extended to William Bergesen, who graciously allowed photographs of his collection to be included in the book.

Contents

Introduction

Dining rooms in the nineteenth century served an important purpose in the Victorian household. Masculine spaces, they were typically filled with solid, heavily carved sideboards and tables, and draped with rich, velvet curtains. Sideboards "groaned" with the weight of opulent, silver serving pieces, set off by the jewel-like tones of colored art glass vases and bowls. There never could be too many objects; after all, these were rooms that were meant to impress.

The following is a visual journey through the recreation of just such a late nineteenth century dining room. We pay particular attention to some of the more unusual curiosities that Victorian tastemakers would have included on their table or sideboard. And isn't this what makes collecting Victoriana so enjoyable today, these whimsical, beautiful, and sometimes even bizarre products of that inventive and colorful time?

Please note that unless identified otherwise, objects are from the late quarter of the nineteenth century, and from the author's collection and that of William Bergesen.

Chapter One:

Setting the Sideboard

Every Victorian dining room had at least one sideboard, and often several (I have three in my dining room!) Sideboards were essential for displaying the beautiful silver and multi-hued art glass that Victorians loved to collect. And of course the storage below was helpful for the many plates and dishes required for a full, Victorian meal. Often set off by beveled glass mirrors, sideboards were frequently embellished with carvings of game and fowl, thought appropriate subjects for stimulating the appetite. Everything from serving dishes in their gleaming, silver stands, to oddities from figural knife rests to pink, porcelain tipplers for serving wine would be displayed with pride. A good rule of thumb to follow when setting up your sideboard is to have a variety of silverplate and glass on view. If the entire surface is covered with only cranberry glass, for example, the effect can be less rich and visually stimulating. Mix the cranberry glass with an assortment of silverplate and other objects for a more interesting setting. And try changing the arrangement periodically, perhaps for the Holidays (changing the arrangement is also a good way to make yourself dust!).

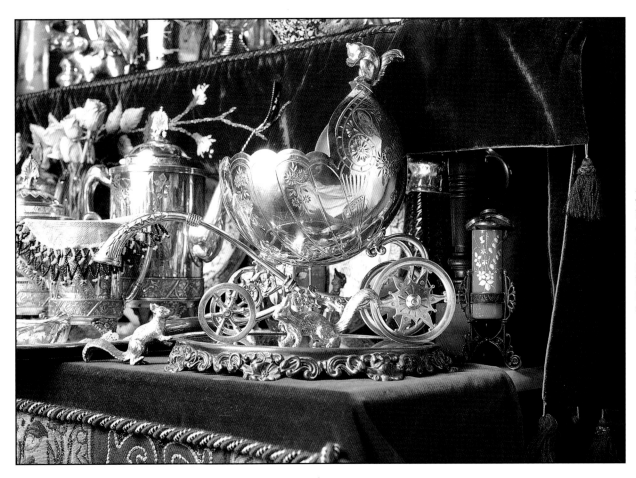

An unusual wheeled chariot nut bowl rests on the corner of the buffet. Circa 1875 to 1880, this nut bowl would have been favored by the gentlemen of the house given its sporting theme.

A silverplate tea service sits in the center of the buffet and is surrounded by decorative silverplate and glassware.

Selected values:
Wheeled chariot nut bowl, $2500;
Silverplate tea service c.1880, $750

Detail of the sideboard shows the intricately embroidered, velvet runner protecting its marble surface. The large Conquistador is actually a lamp.

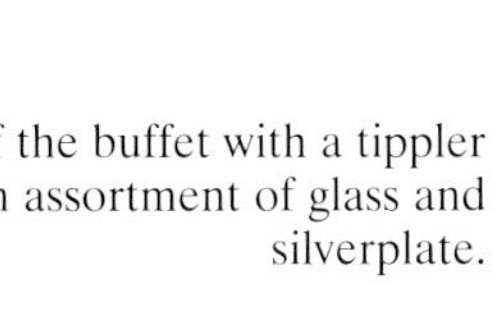

The corner of the buffet with a tippler and an assortment of glass and silverplate.

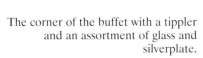

Value: Conquistador lamp, $7500

The Flying Pegasus is the name of this Meriden, silverplate tippler. Note the storks engraved on the body of the tippler.

Detail of the Flying Pegasus tippler – note the three-dimensional stork with a fish caught in its beak in the drip pan underneath.

Values: Flying pegasus tippler, $5000

A castor set with its original decorated glass bottles is always a find.

An elegant, soup tureen with a classical bust as its finial.

alues: Castor set with original bottles, $1800; Soup reen with classical bust, $1200

An unusual pickle caster of pressed glass in the form of a castle.

An exotic pickle castor in the form of two Mary Gregory girls standing on a flying Persian carpet boasts its original, hand-painted, glass insert.

Values: Castle pickle castor, $1200; Mary Gregory pickle castor: $1800

Cats and cream are inseparable in these two creamers.

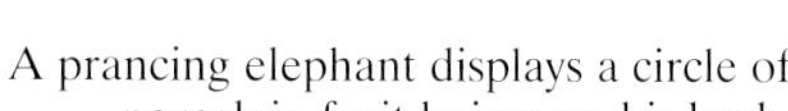

A prancing elephant displays a circle of porcelain fruit knives on his back.

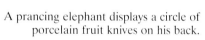

alues: Cat creamers, $750; Elephant knife holder, $800

Everything from an elaborate porcelain and silverplate tippler to a large silverplate soccer trophy is proudly displayed, including multicolored Victorian glass.

A hand-painted, porcelain tippler rests in an ornate, silverplate frame.

A pink porcelain tippler sits amid Victorian art glass on the sideboard. Note the tippler's ornate spout.

Detail of the tippler, which is hand-painted with fat robins and flowers.

Values: Hand-painted porcelain tipplers, $2500

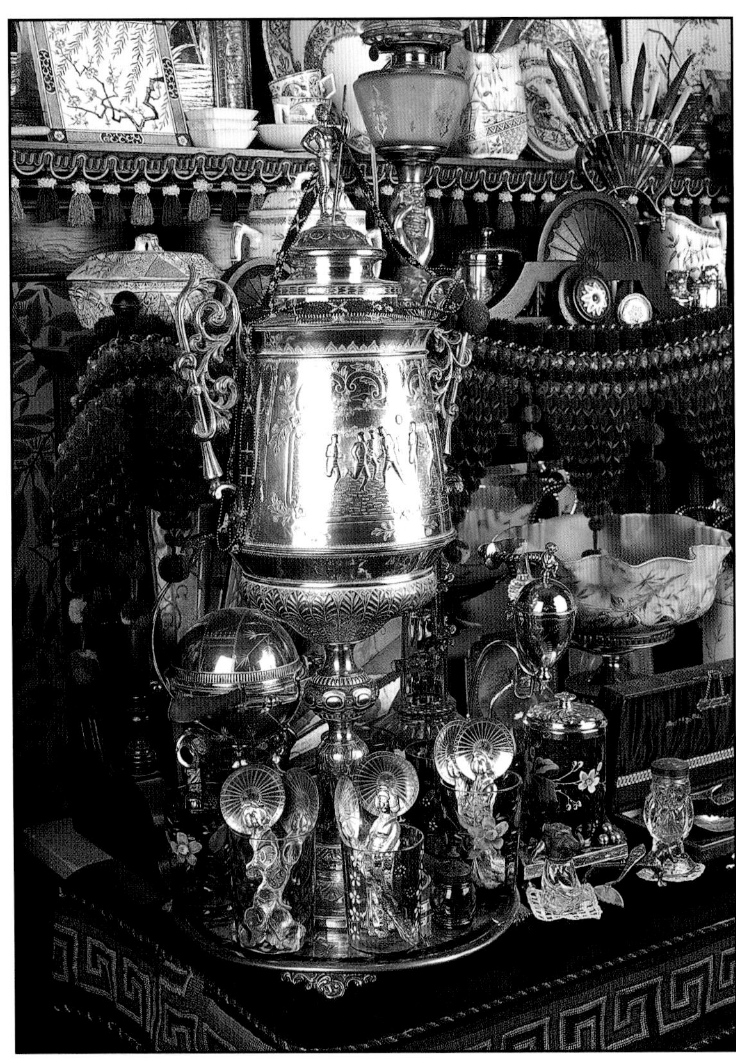

The large trophy is surrounded by colored, enameled glasses holding sterling silver serving spoons in the form of Geisha girls.

Trophy detail.

Value: Silverplate trophy, $1800

This nut bowl takes the form of a lovely gilt-lined silver basket, decorated with squirrels along its rim.

Of course, a squirrel knife rest is needed to display nutpicks, used with a nutcracker to open the nuts. This nut bowl features intricate Eastlake designs and is elevated on its own pedestal.

Values: Silver basket nutbowl, $1200; Eastlake nutbowl, $1500

The built-in sideboard showcases an assortment of Victorian silverplate and glassware. The robin's egg blue, beaded fringe across the bottom is a colorful accent.

Silverplate and cranberry glass crowd another corner of the buffet. Colorful accents include vintage Victorian textiles such as the beaded firescreen and robin's-egg-blue, beaded shelf liner.

A grouping of etched glass serving pieces, silverplate, and richly hued glassware on the buffet.

Serving butter with style was the purpose of this ornate, late nineteenth century butter dish.

alue: Ornate butter dish, $800

Double pickle castors are unusual. The round etched glass bottle, in its original holder, held condiments.

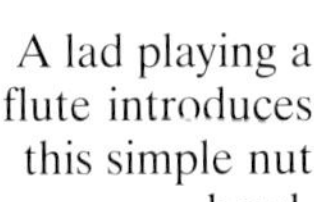

A lad playing a flute introduces this simple nut bowl.

Values: Condiment holder, $750; Double pickle castor, $1200; Lad and lute nutbowl, $1500

An elaborately engraved tippler set with its two goblets still intact.

An unusual nut bowl features a happy squirrel with his nut, sitting atop an enameled glass bowl.

ılues: Tippler and stand, $1500; Glass and ver frame nutbowl, $850

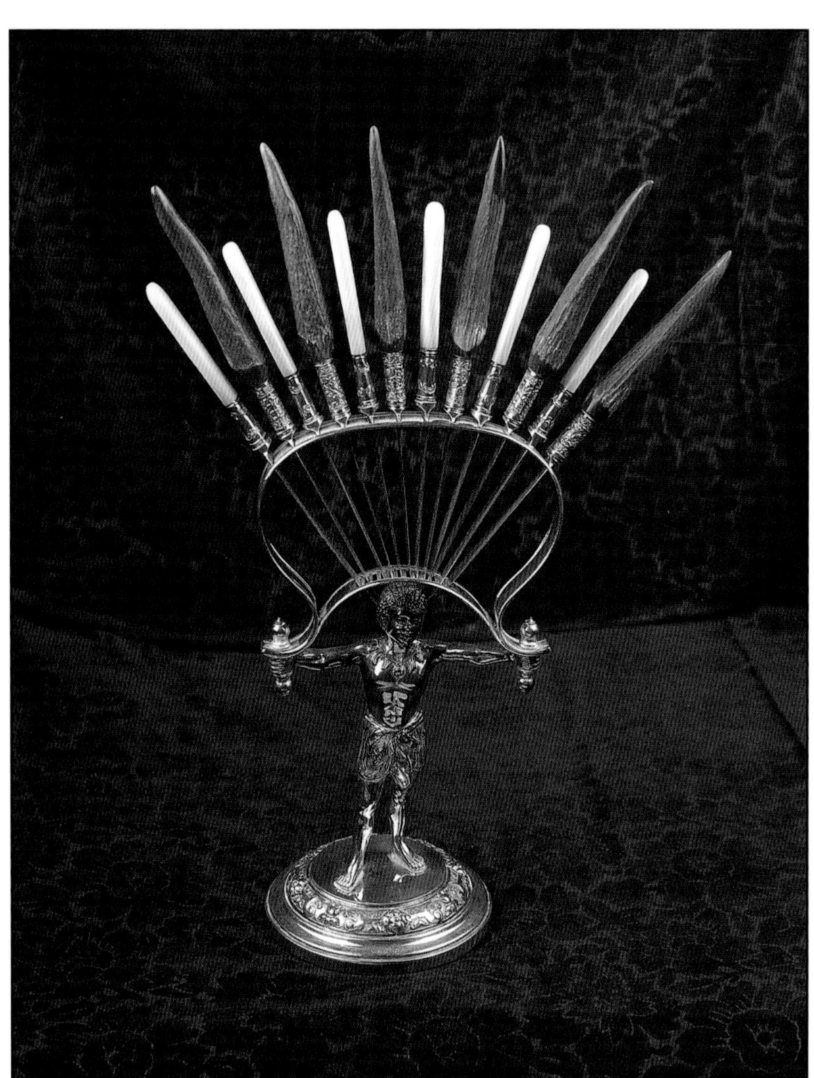

Figural knife rests would display your fruit knives in style, as this black figure shows.

Unusual, root beer hobnail glass makes up the body of this lovely ice water pitcher.

Values: Black figural knife rest, $750; Hobnail glass ice pitcher, $1200

The Barge of Venus was an elaborate centerpiece (meant to hold fruit or flowers) made by Meriden for the 1893 Chicago World's Fair. A gallant cherub guides his gilded barge, pulled by two elegant swans, through a pond of lilies and cattails.

Cherub musicians playing a harp and flute serenade the barge along its journey.

alue: Barge of Venus centerpiece, $7500

A pink, cased glass ice bucket has silverplate icicles hanging from its edges.

Lorne, an 1847 Rogers Brothers Silverplate pattern, circa 1885, had many interesting serving pieces available, from pudding spoons to ice tongs.

Values: Pink, cased glass ice bucket, $1200; Lorne silverplate serving pieces, $200-$500

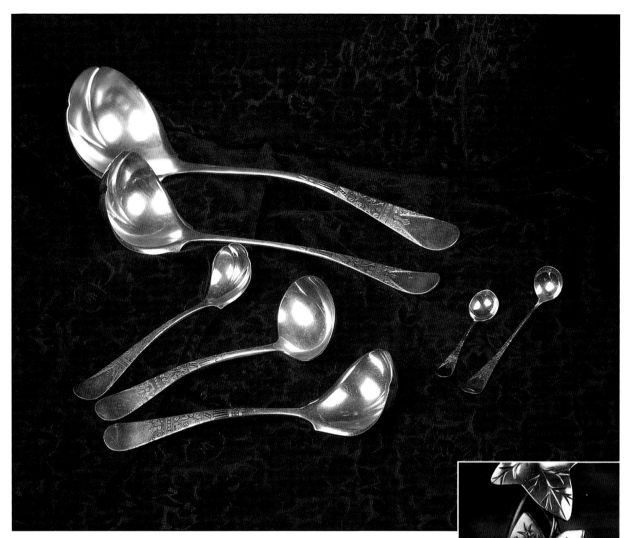

Serving ladles included, from the smallest to the largest, mustard, cream, soup, oyster, and punch.

A close-up view of the previous spoon reveals a fly climbing across the leaves of its handle.

A spoon warmer in the shape of a shell would warm the serving spoon with hot water.

Values: Silverplate serving ladles, $200 - $500; Spoon warmer, $750

Beneath the sideboard: plates, cups, and serving pieces in the nineteenth century pattern "Rustic."

Detail of the Rustic pattern.

Discovering a set of silver in its original presentation case is always a lucky find. Fontainebleau is an 1880s sterling pattern by Gorham.

lue: Fontainebleau serving set in box, $2000

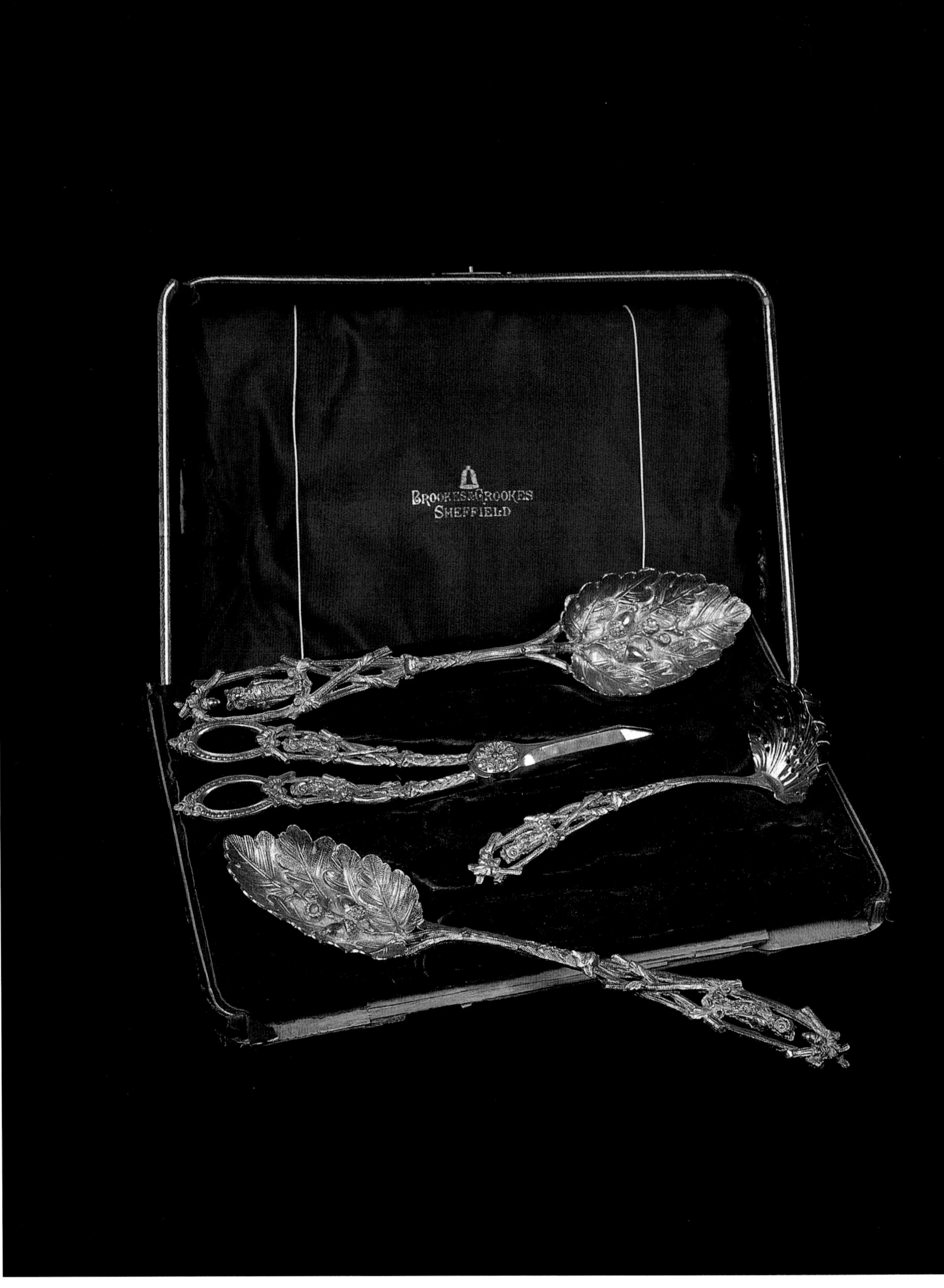

A wonderful, boxed grape or fruit set with shears, spoons, and ladle, decorated with a pensive owl on its handle.

Chapter Two:

Serving Pieces From Soup to Nuts

Every Victorian meal, breakfast through supper, used a variety of serving pieces for a richer, more interesting presentation. Breakfast, for example, had everything from handsome, transferware, cooked egg holders, to condiment sets topped by squirrels or a knight. Or how about a sterling, gold washed orange half holder? The sky was the limit for nut bowls (nuts were considered a healthy food for breakfast, lunch as well as dinner by Victorian physicians) and everything from squirrels to nymphs could be found riding atop the nuts. And don't forget that a properly set table in Victorian times would often have two soup tureens, one for each end of the table; the decorations on the soup tureen finials said to represent the type of soup served.

1847 Rogers Brothers, Lorne pattern silverplate was made in everything from pastry forks to cake slicers.

Geisha girl sterling serving spoons.

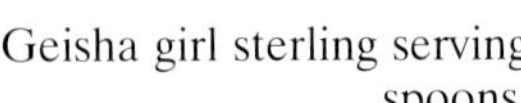

Values: Geisha girl sterling spoons, $750 apiece

Colored glass fairy lamps and a nut bowl with a glass-eyed robin rest on the top of the sideboard.

A fat and sassy robin with glass eyes roosts atop this nut bowl in the form of an egg.

Value: Robin nutbowl, $1750

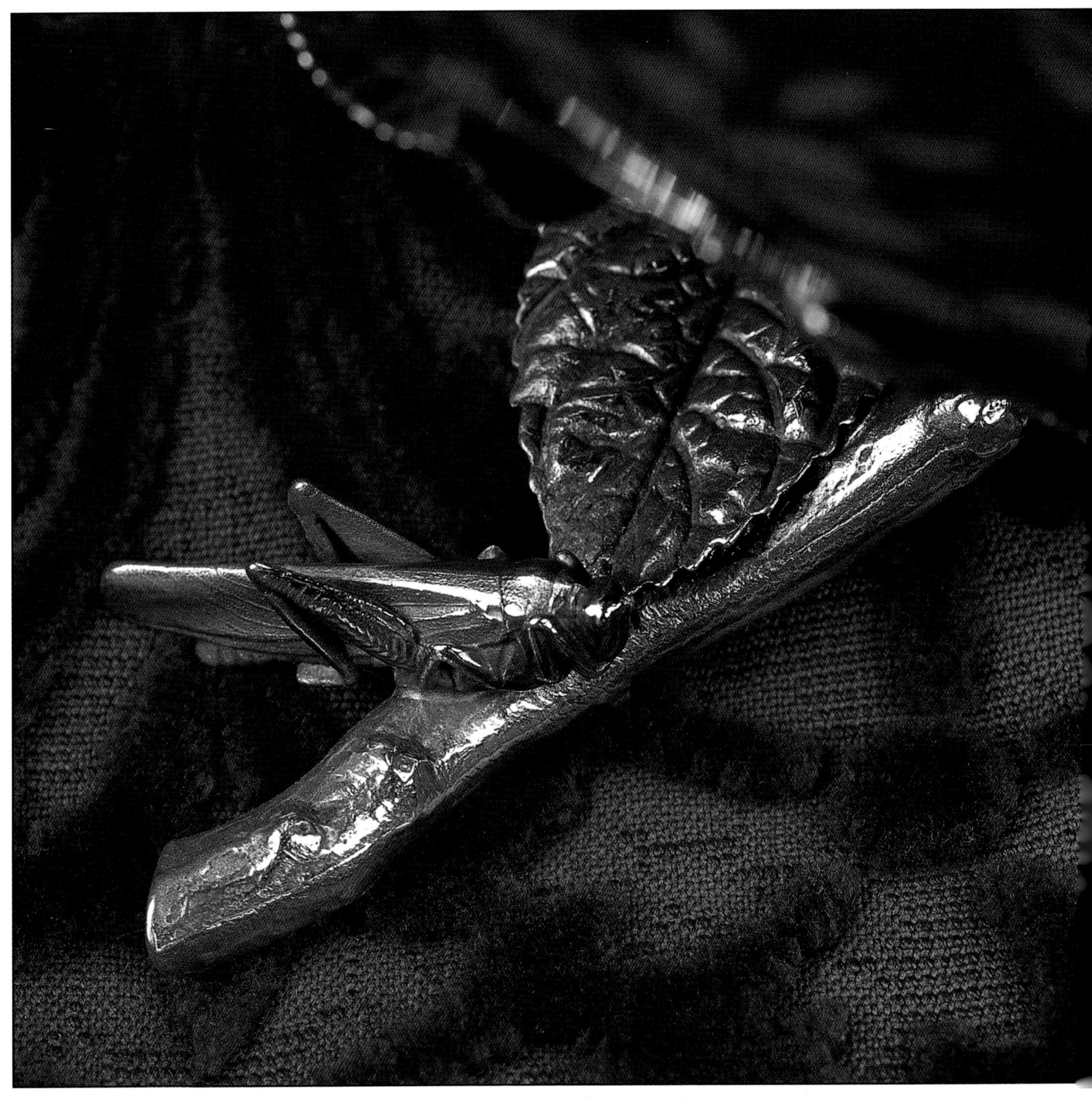

Detail of the robin nut bowl showing a grasshopper climbing up its leg.

Opposite page: A boy balances a baton atop this doub
spooner, circa 1880, which rotates to help the din
make his selectio

Value, opposite page: Double spooner with boy, $750

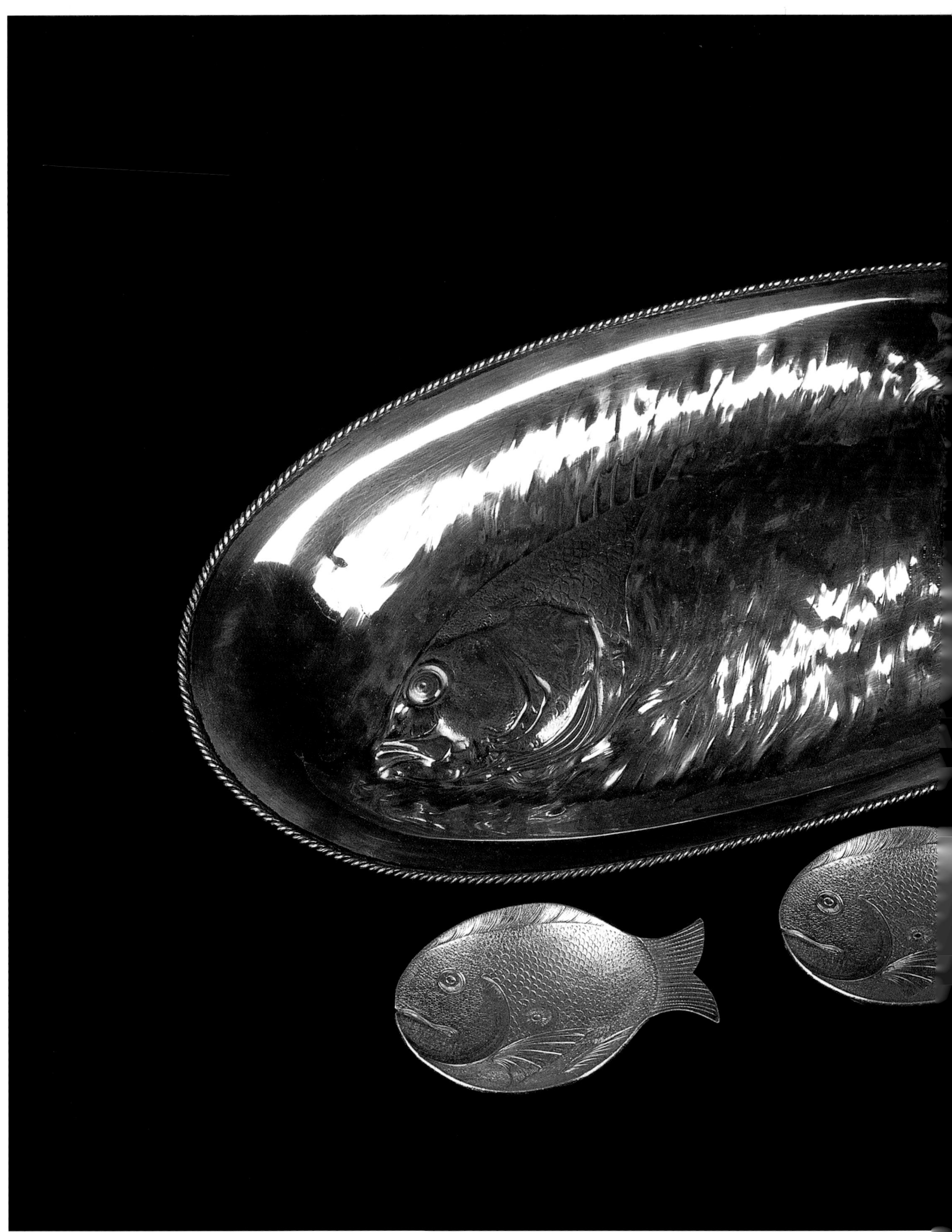

A Tufts serving dish for fish features a three-dimensional fish, and is surrounded by Tufts, fish-shaped butter pats.

lues: Tufts serving dish for fish, $750; Tufts fish butter
ts: $250 apiece; Grotesque fish water pitcher, $1200

An amusing, hand-painted water pitcher with a band of grotesque fish swimming across its body.

Detail of the humorous fish.

The plate rail holds an assortment of brown and white transferware and Victorian accents.

A collection of spooners, the ones on the ends even have bells to call the servant.

Another spooner, and a spoon warmer (filled with hot water to warm your spoon before using it).

Values: Spooners, $500-$750

An elegant, circa 1875 wine set in its original silver-plated holder. The leaded glass bottles are delicately etched, as are the wine glasses.

A castor set with rare, ruby glass bottles.

Selected Values: Ruby bottles castor set: $1500

A Victorian casserole has a removable porcelain liner.

Delicate flowers and birds are engraved on the lid of this silverplate casserole.

Value: Victorian casserole, $250

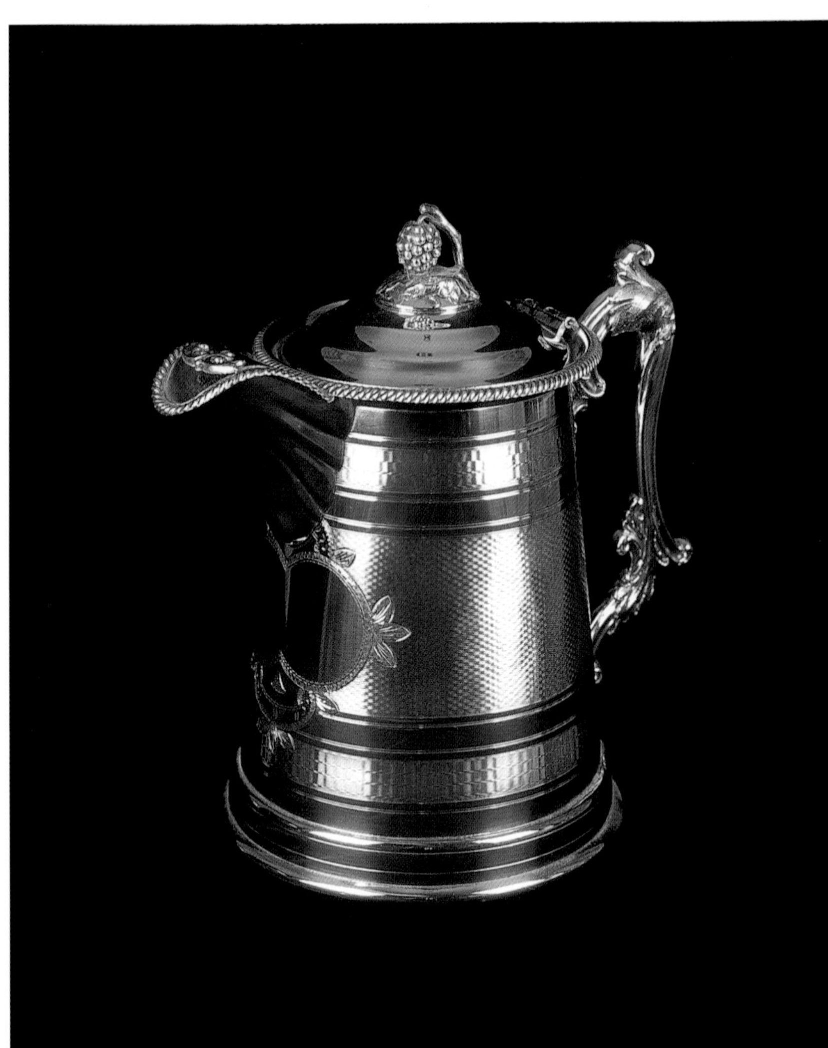

An elegant ice water pitcher with more restrained engraving, circa 1890.

Cruet sets were used for every meal, holding condiments such as oil, vinegar, and mustard. Breakfast sets were typically smaller and often featured a theme, such as this set in the shape of a horseshoe, which implied good luck.

Values: Ice water pitcher, $750; Horseshoe cruet set, $800

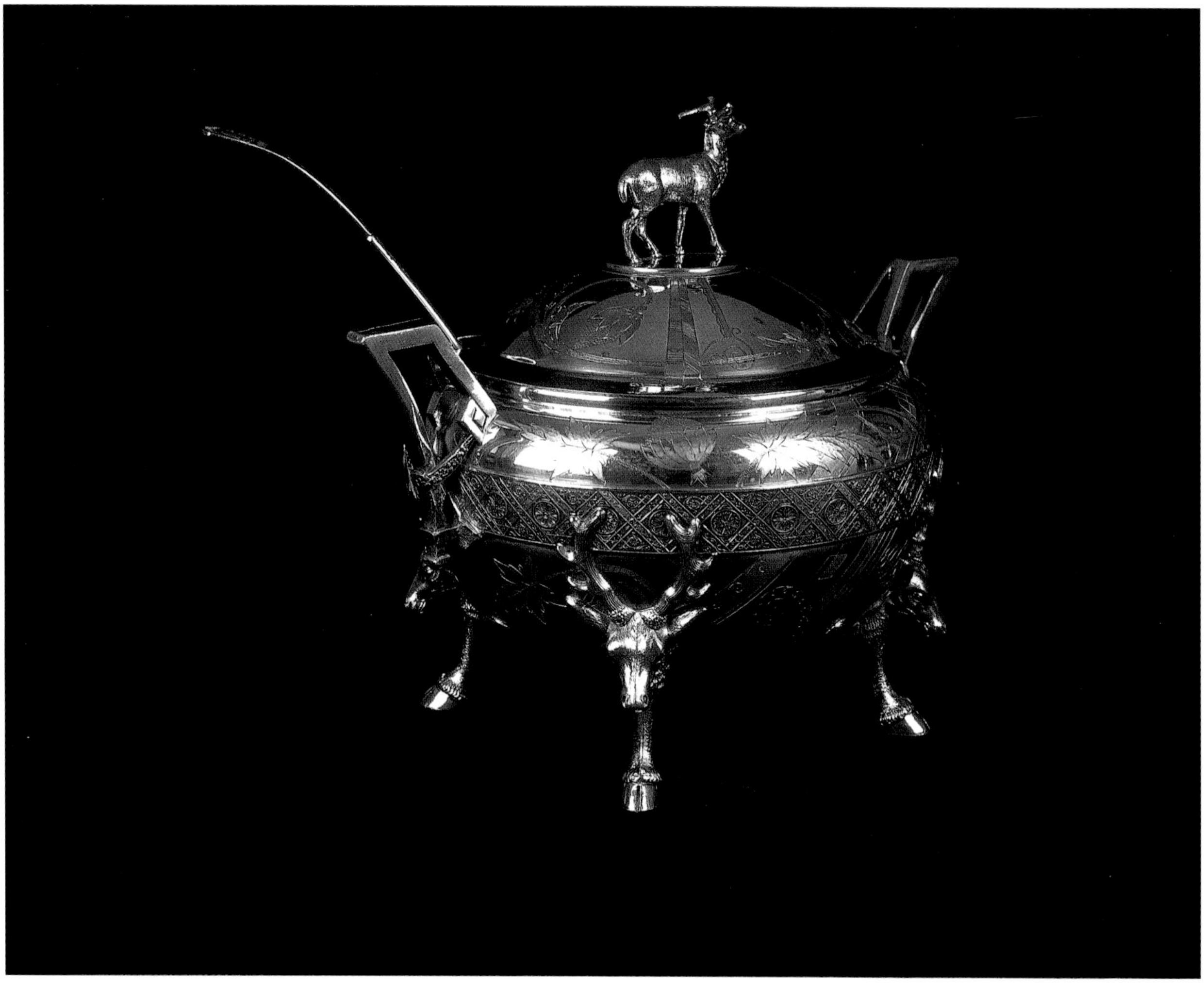

A soup tureen
[wi]th a deer on top
[a]nd stags for legs.
It was said that
[t]he design of the
tureen was to be
an indication of
the type of soup
being served.

Ice water could be served in a variety of ornate silverplate pitchers.

Selected value: Deer soup tureen, $1500

A hard-to-find, half-waiter tray with an Aesthetic pattern of bamboo and fans rests in this corner of the plate rail. The paper owl fan was from the 1893 Chicago World's Fair. Tassels were added along the entire length of the plate rail for more color and detail.

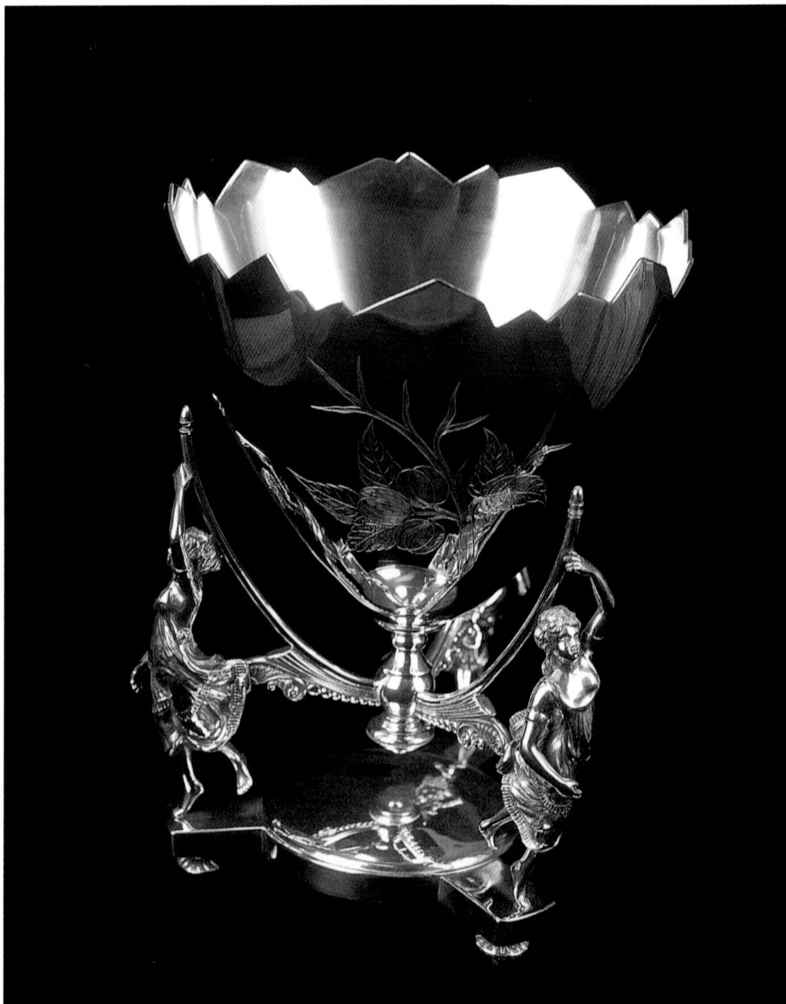

A trio of dancing maidens holds this nut bowl aloft.

Values: Half-waiter tray, $2500; Dancing maidens nutbowl, $1500

Lobster was served in its own, gold-washed bowl, with of course a curious lobster crawling along it top.

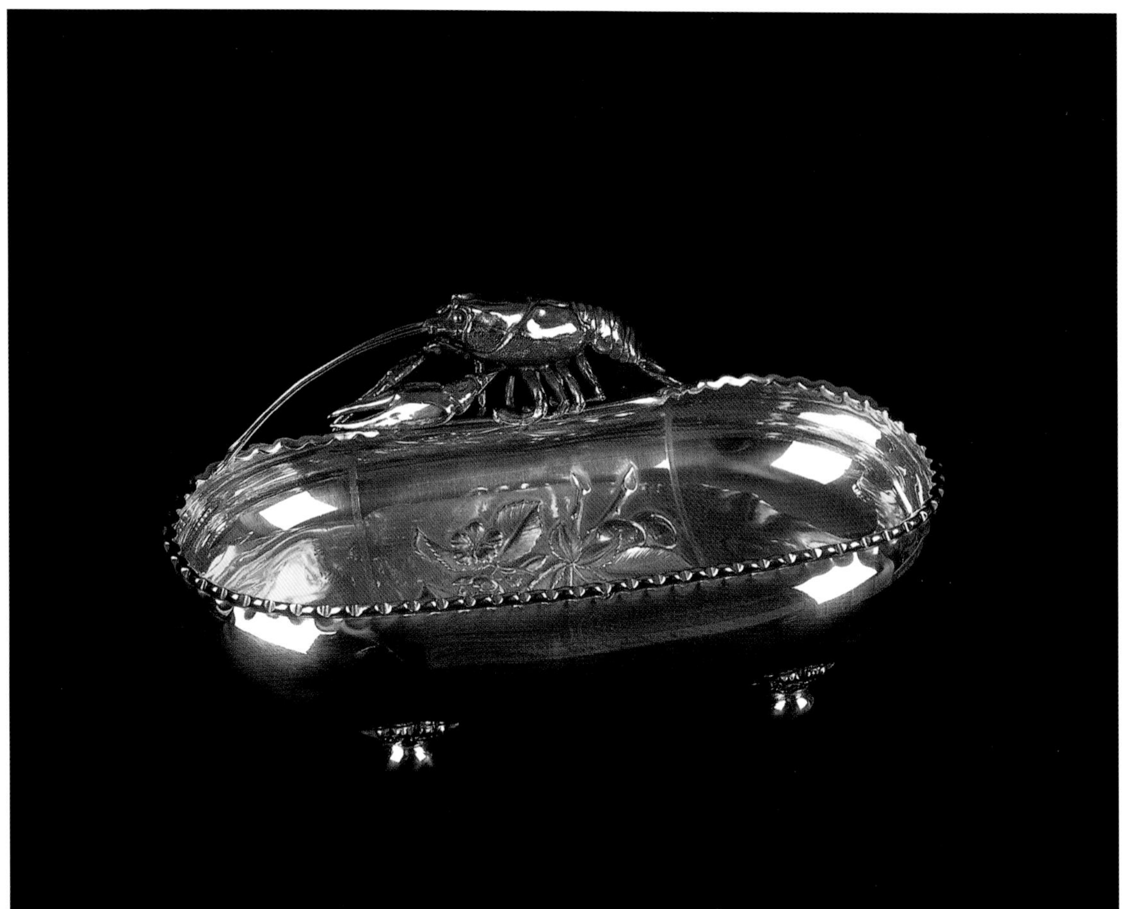

A bookcase stores figural soup tureens among paintings and leather-bound volumes.

Values: Lobster bowl, $800

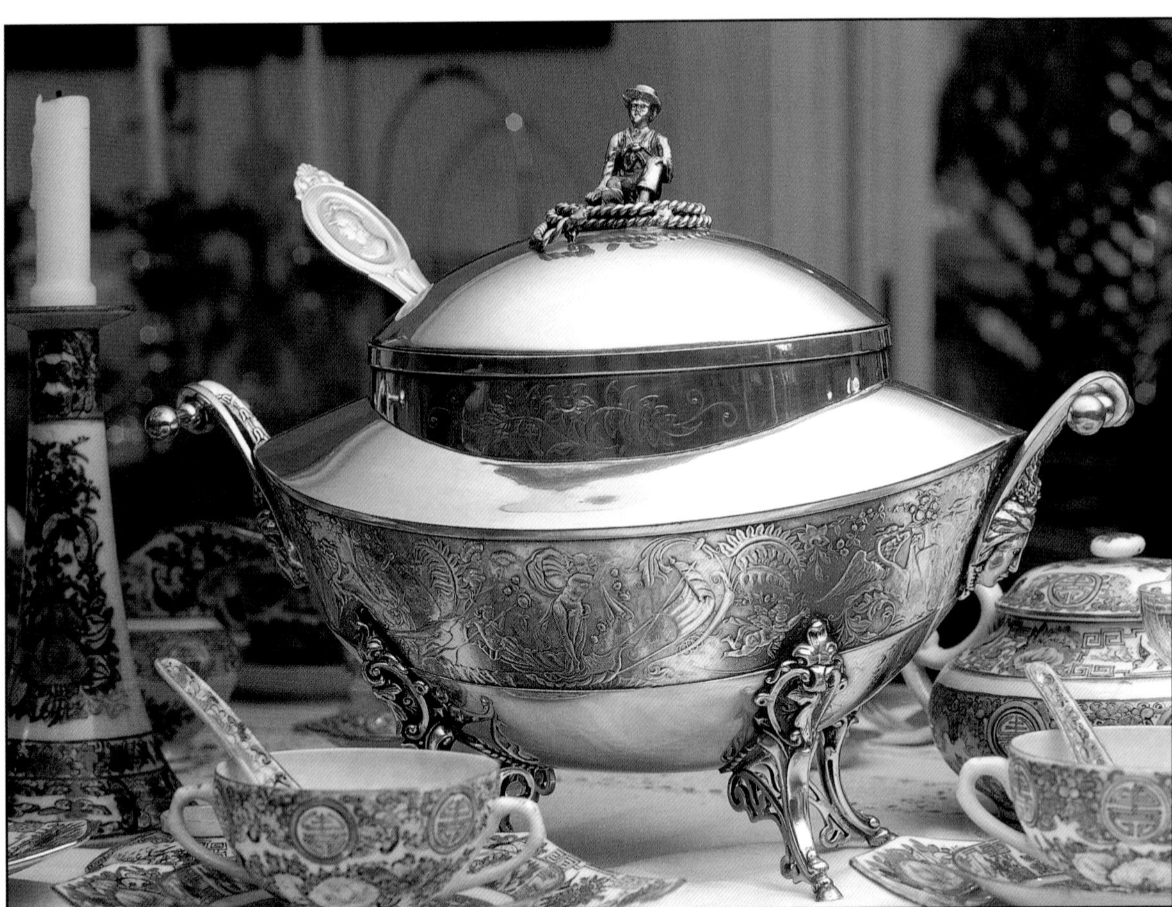

A little boy rests atop this soup tureen, which is set on a table with nineteenth century Rose Medallion china.

Mary Gregory figures cavort around the bottom of this butter dish, while butter pats in the form of Japanese fans are ready to hold the butter.

Values: Little boy soup tureen, $1800; Mary Gregory butter dish, $1500; Japanese fans butter pats, $75 apiece

A butter dish with an engraved scene beneath the glass. The butter pats are Eastlake designs.

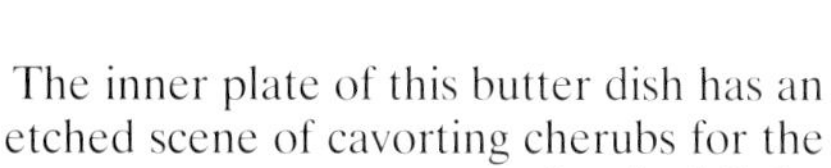

The inner plate of this butter dish has an etched scene of cavorting cherubs for the diner's delight.

es: Engraved butter dish, $750; Eastlake butter pats, $50 apiece

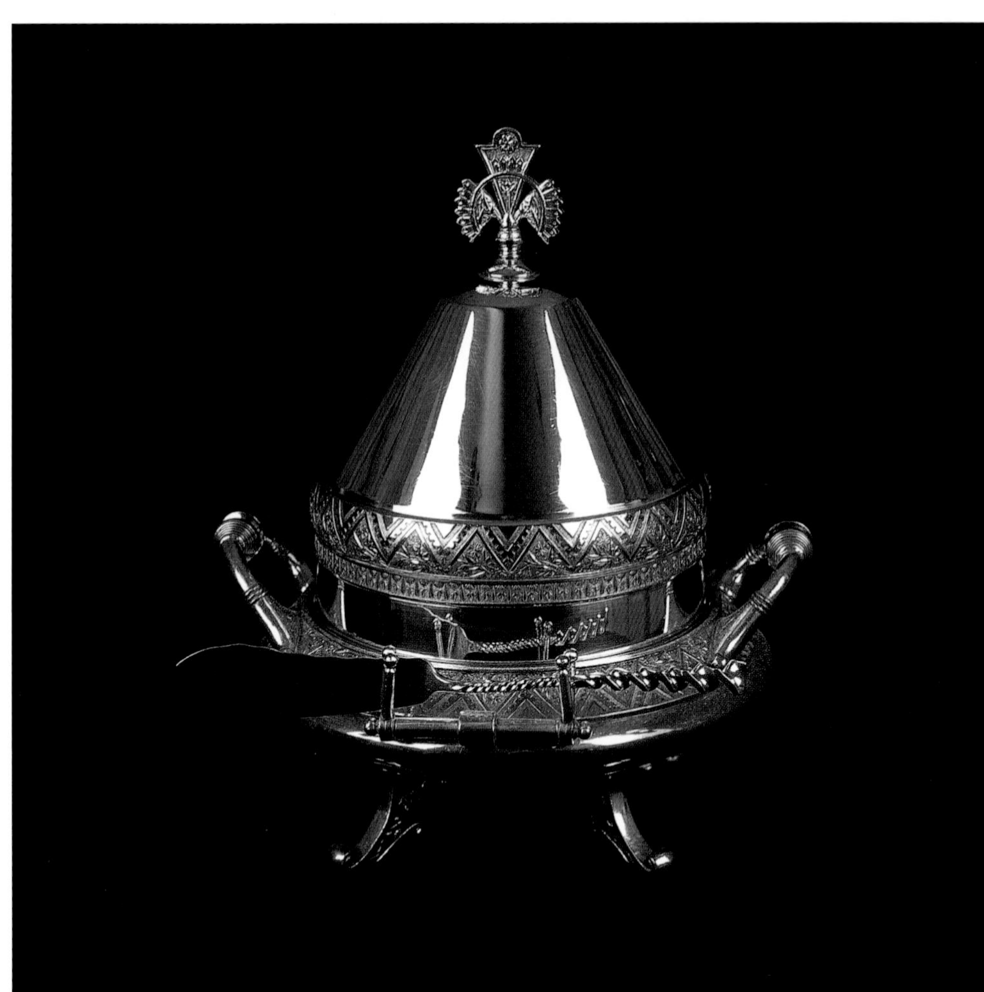

A butter dish with a Turkish design.

A butter dish with a cow finial features intricate engraving beneath its glass tray.

Values: Turkish butter dish, $750; Cow butter dish, $500

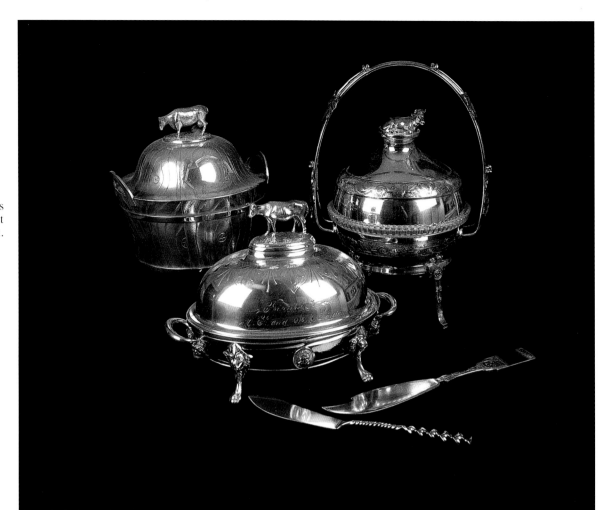

Butter dishes with cows as finials are the most common.

An early butter dish in the form of an acorn that rotates, this dish featured a compartment for ice above the butter. Not very efficient for cooling the butter, this model did not last long on the market and is now a rare collectible.

Value: Acorn butter dish, $1750

The acorn butter dish closed. A butter knife keeps its doors shut.

An ornate and unusual, silverplate punch bowl is guarded by a finial of a little boy carrying a barrel over his back.

Value: Silverplate punch bowl, $2000

Elegant egg cups with gilded interiors rest on their own stand.

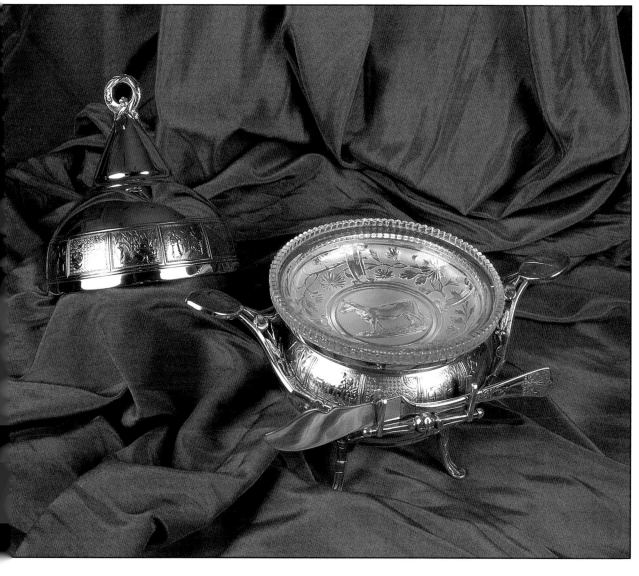

A stately cow is engraved beneath the glass of this butter dish.

Value: Egg cups and holder, $500

Butter dishes featured many designs, such as this acorn, with a squirrel on its top. Butter pats to hold the butt have an Eastlake design, while the butter knife rests on a squirrel knife rest.

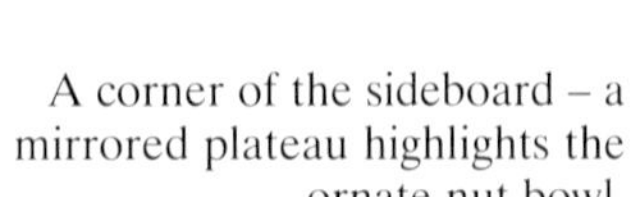

A corner of the sideboard – a mirrored plateau highlights the ornate nut bowl.

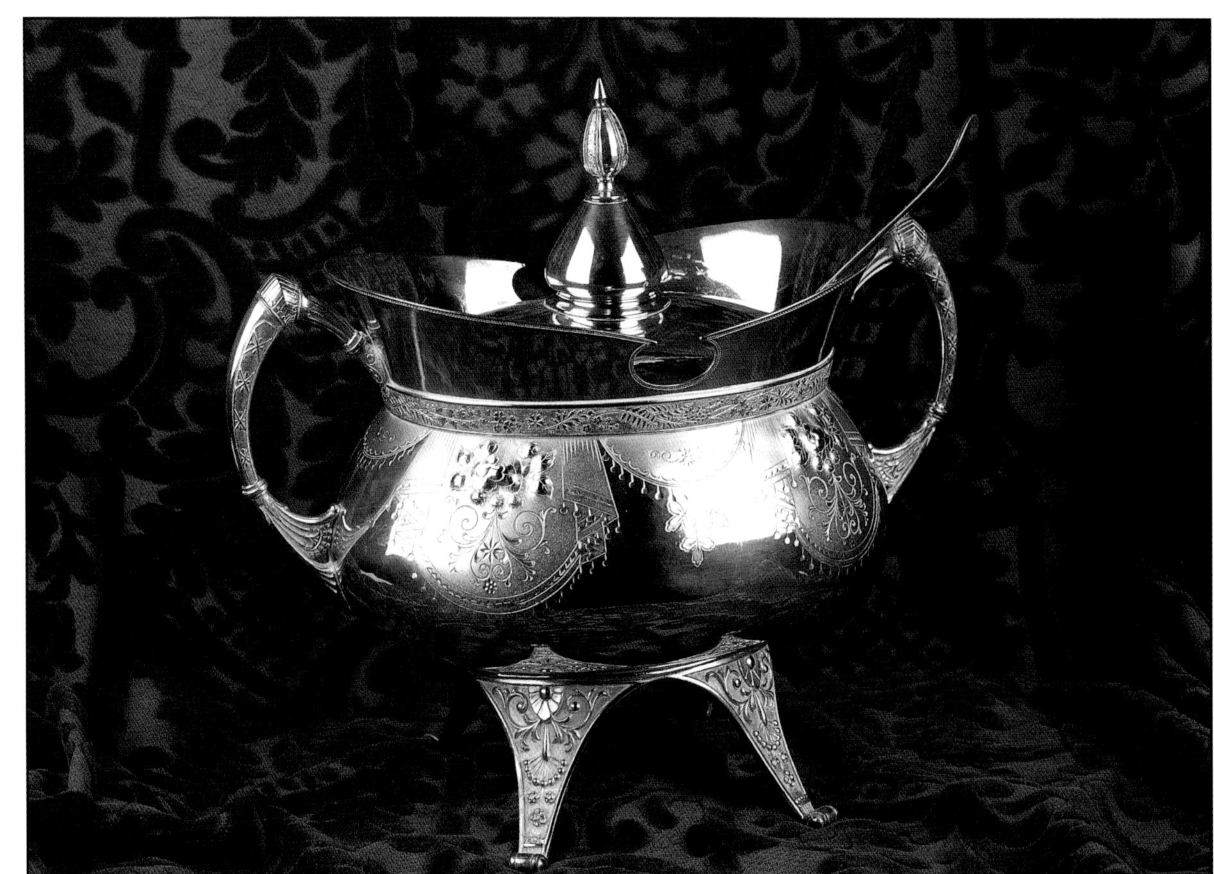
An Eastlake soup tureen with ornate engraving, circa 1880.

Detail of the Eastlake soup tureen, showing the intricate pattern of folds of drapes.

Value: Eastlake soup tureen, $1250

A spout in the form of a bearded man's head sets of this cranberry glass decanter.

A striking compote with stylized griffins along its legs.

Values, this page: Cranberry decanter, $800; Griffin compote, $1750. Opposite page: Asparagus tongs, $250 apiece; Silverplate tray with cattails, $800

Individual asparagus tongs; the Victorian diner would never navigate a slippery piece of asparagus with just a fork!

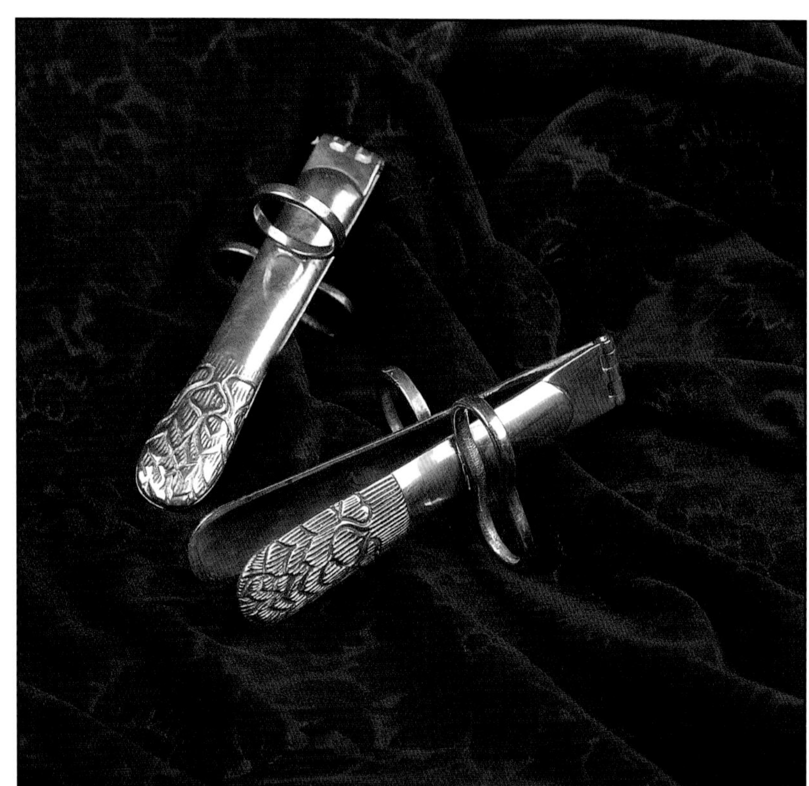

A silverplate serving tray engraved with cattails and a stork, a favorite Victorian motif, rests on the plate rail.

An elegant sugar bowl.

Value: Sugar bowl, $7

Chapter Three:

Time for Tea

Tea was an important ritual in Victorian times, a time out in a busy day to socialize and relax before a strenuous evening began. The mistress of the house had an opportunity to show off her handiwork to her friends, and would often serve tea with hand embroidered linens, while covering the silver teapot with a needlepoint, perhaps even beaded tea cozy. Nothing escaped the fertile, Victorian imagination – even the tea caddies were designed with flair, such as one in the form of a rhinoceros.

Tea time implements including a hand-embroidered tea cozy and rhinoceros tea caddy rest on a table in front of the ornate Victorian velvet draperies. The window shade is painted with a scene of the front garden gate.

A rare Meriden silverplate calling card table was originally meant to receive a guest's calling cards and now serves as a table for tea.

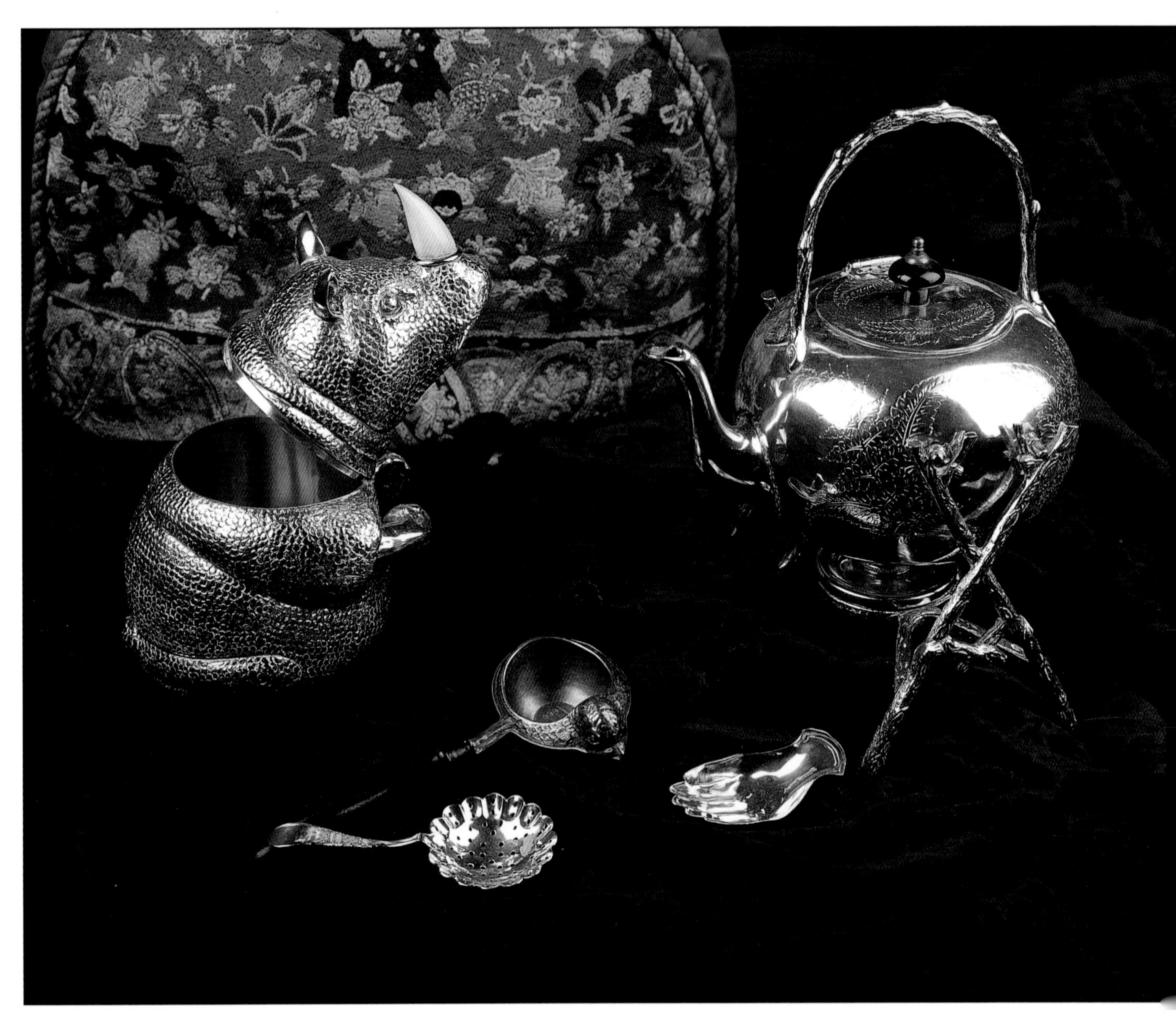

A hand-embroidered tea cozy would keep this kettle warm if its burner was not used.

Selected values, previous page: Meriden silverplate calling card table, $10,000; this page: Rhinoceros Tea Caddy, $1200

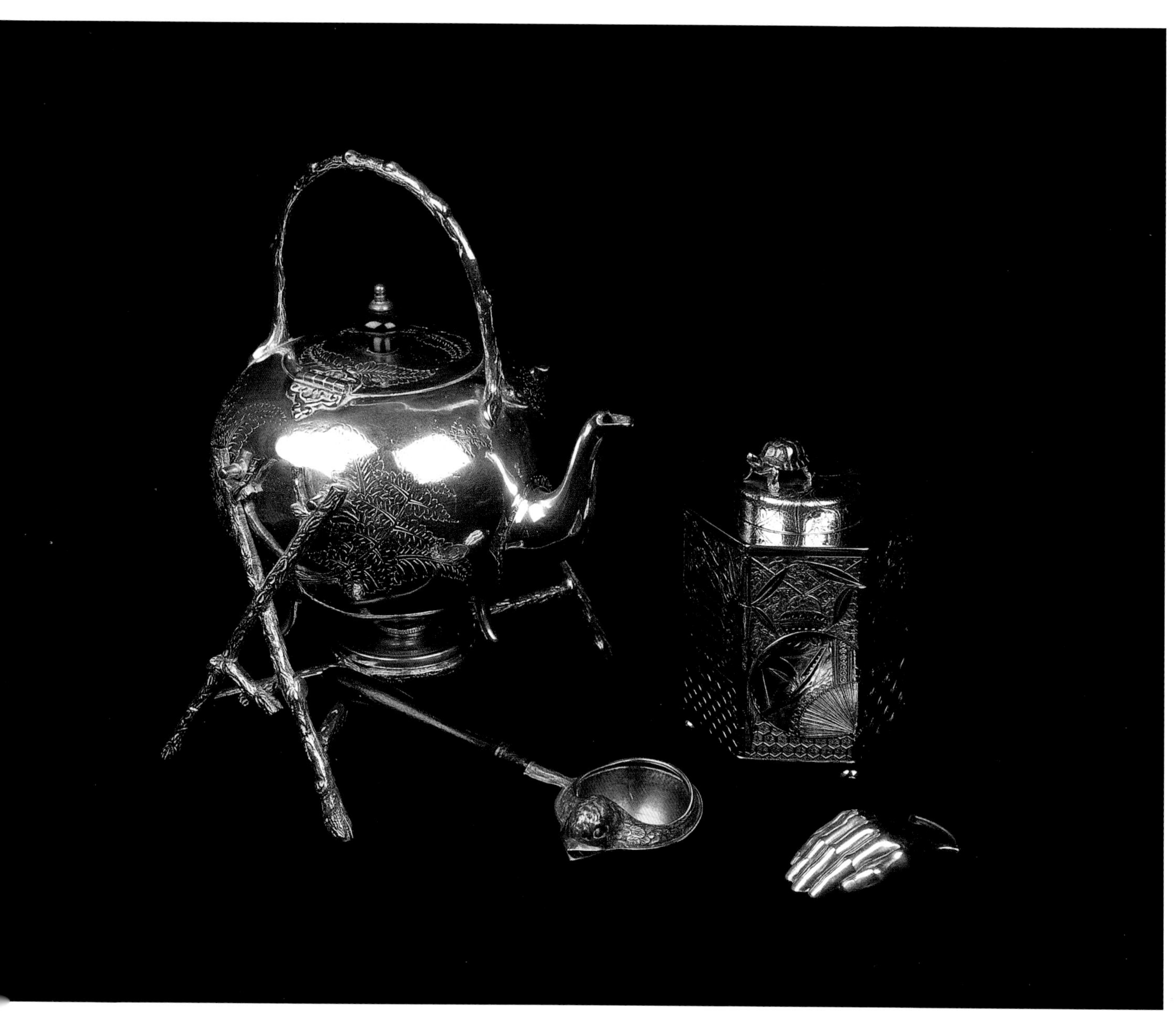

Victorian implements for tea include a teapot with its own burner beneath, a tea leaf strainer in the form of a swallow, a tea caddy, and even a hand used to scoop out the tea leaves.

Values: Teapot with burner, $300; Swallow tea leaf strainer, $350; Hand tea scoop, $250

A tea service with elaborate engraving an Eastlake pattern.

Tea time necessitated utensils for straining the tea leaves, such as these spoons, which would rest over the teacup, or the long strainer, meant to go down the spout of the teapot. The pointed end could break up the tea leaves, while the slotted bowl could strain the leaves as the hostess poured. The silver-plated hand was actually a handy scoop for the tea.

small whisk brush r the table, this was lso a tricky way for e maid to sneak in a swig or two while e cleaned up. Note that the top is tually a bottle with a screw-on lid. The graving on the side f the brush gives it away ("Just a few swallows").

An Aesthetic silver-plated tea caddy has an Oriental motif with a turtle atop its lid.

Values, opposite page: Long-handled tea Strainer, $250; Spoon tea strainers, $200. This page: Whisk brush bottle, $250; Aesthetic tea caddy, $1200

Medieval characters stroll across this tea caddy.

An unusual tea pot called the "Self Pouring" model, the tea would be forced out of the spout as the lid was lowered.

Values: Medieval tea caddy, $250; Self-Pouring Tea Pot, $750

Tea pots include a whimsical transferware pot with birds, and an Anglo-Japanese designed English pot with a matching underplate. The slotted spoon is for straining tea.

A Turkish-style coffee set, circa 1880.

Values: Transferware tea pots, $750 apiece; Turkish coffee set, $800

Biscuit jars with hand-painted designs were used to pass biscuits during tea or dessert.

A table set for tea.

Value, above photo : Porcelain biscuit jars, $750 apiece

Chapter Four:

Glassware

Victorian glass was rich and colorful, a rainbow of ruby reds, opalescent greens, and robin's egg blues. A successful Victorian dining room should always have a nice assortment of colorful glass to add interest, from a cranberry epergne on the table or sideboard to Early American Pressed Glass goblets set around the table. Hand decorated glass is always the most desirable, especially the gilded and enameled examples.

The built-in buffet sparkles with a collection of Victorian, enameled cranberry and opalescent glass.

Storks were a favorite Victorian motif, as seen in this assortment of vases and glasses.

Exquisitely hand-painted glasses by Moser, a well-known nineteenth century Bohemian art glass manufacturer, feature storks and lilies.

pposite page: Cranberry glass vases, decorated with hand-ainted dogwoods and a water carafe of rich red cranberry ass are beautiful on either the sideboard or the dining table.

Values, opposite page: Pair of cranberry glass vases, $1800; cranberry water carafe, $800. This page: Moser glasses, $800 apiece.

Cranberry glass epergnes and vases look good with silver on the table. The napkin rings are porcelain and feature initials of the diners. The painted ball on top of the vase is a Victorian whimsy meant to keep out the flies.

A bride's basket with a cranberry ruffled glass bowl.

Values, Cranberry glass epergne, $750; Porcelain napkin rings, $250 apiece; Cranberry bride's basket, $750

A striking bride's basket with a Coralene bowl in a seaweed design.

Victorians loved color. Here a pair of brightly colored turquoise Bristol glass lusters is shown with a similarly colored epergne, featuring two cherubs guarding a glass trumpet adorned with hand-painted lilies of the valley.

Values: Coralene bride's basket, $1500; Bristol Glass lustres, $1500; Cherub epergne, $1200

Cranberry glass bells would often be placed on the table to summon the servants. Most were actually quite fragile and only decorative, so a more functional metal bell, such as the one in the center, would actually be used.

Decalomania was a favorite Victorian way of decorating glass with scraps and mementos of loved ones.

ues, opposite page: Cranberry glass bells, $400 to $800;
tal bell, $125. This page: Decalomania, $250 to $500

This nut bowl, circa 1875, is in the form of a seashell, guarded by a winged fairy resting on top. The sparkling silver bowl is the center of a grouping of blue Victorian glassware

Brilliantly hued Victorian art glass suc
as this peachblow Web vase and art
glass vase of a kingfisher add color anc
interest when combined with silverplat

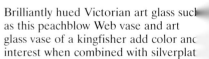

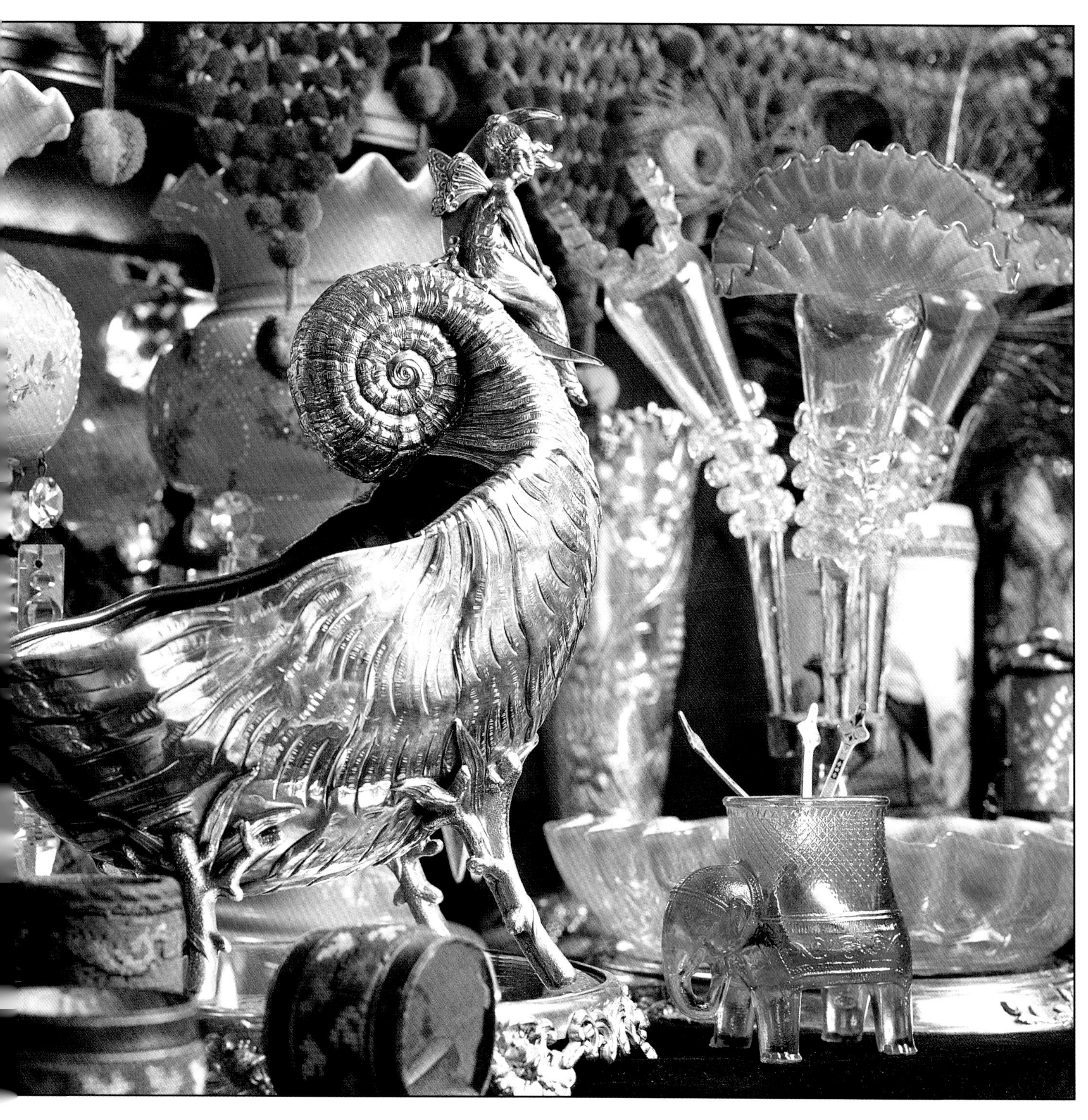

Values, opposite page: Web peachblow Kingfisher vase, $1200; Web swallow vase, $1000. This page: Blue opalescent glass epergne, $1200

A striking bride's basket, held in an ornate silverplate frame, has a pink glas bowl set off by an enameled, apple gree exterior.

Cherubs dance around the base of this beautifully hand-painted, cased glass brides' basket.

Values: Apple green glass bowl bride's basket, $1500; Cherubs and cased glass basket, $2500

A beautiful compote for fruit or flowers, set in an elaborate silverplate frame, still has its original hand-painted bowl.

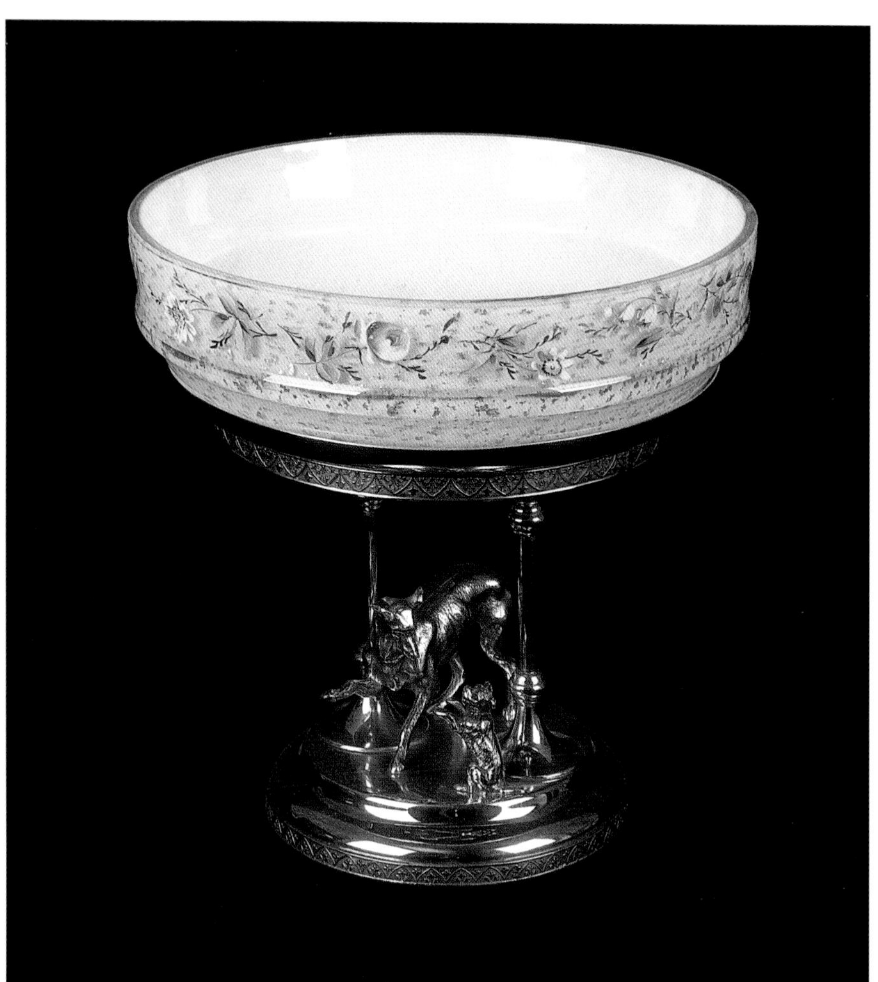

An ornate, gilded and ruffled cranberry glass bride's basket.

Values: Hand-painted bowl fruit compote, $1200; Cranberry glass bride's basket, $800

This bride's basket has a beautiful pink cased glass interior and ornate hand-painted fruit on its exterior.

Two unusual pickle castors. The cranberry glass castor on the left has a compartment for toothpicks above, while the example on the right has its original sapphire-blue glass insert with hand-painted flowers.

Values: Pink cased glass bride's basket, $1200; Pickle castor with toothpick holder, $1500

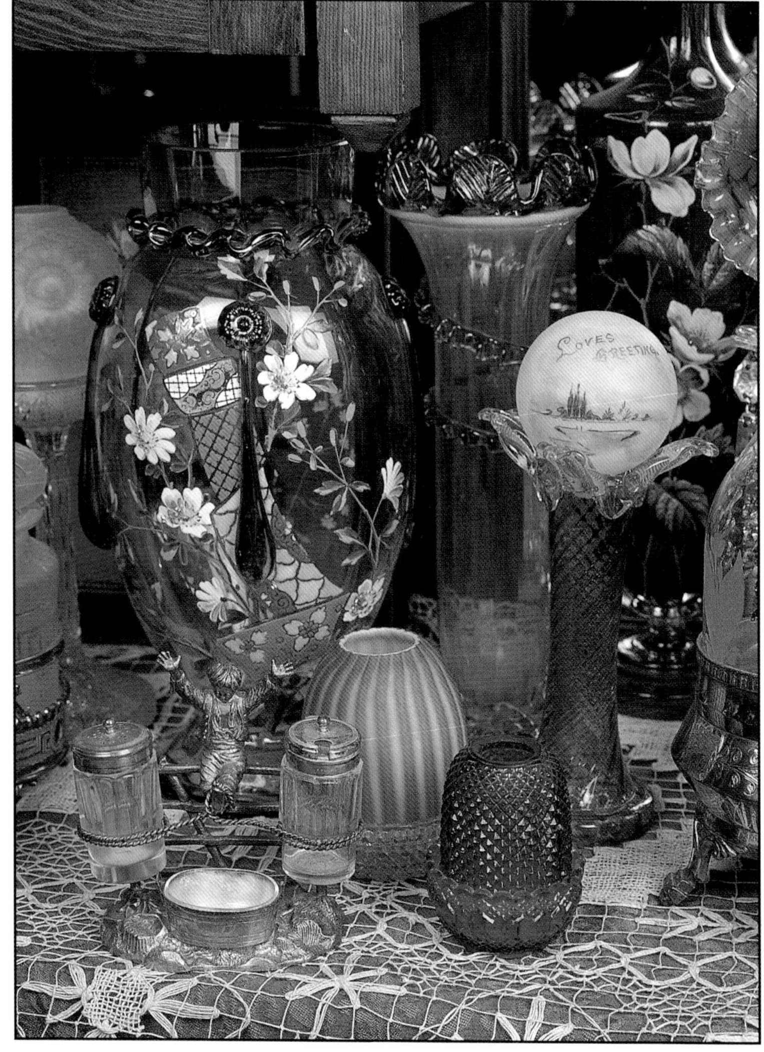

An assortment of Victorian, colored art glass nestles in a corner of the buffet. The hand-painted ball was meant to rest on a creamer to keep out the flies.

Colorful, Victorian witch balls (said to keep away the evil spirits) and smoke bells, used above a chandelier to keep the smoke off the ceiling, form a canopy of glass hanging above the built-in buffet.

Values: Creamer ball, $250; Victorian smoke bells and witch balls, $250 to $750

Delicately painted flowers adorn this amber vase, which is set off by an elaborate silverplate stand.

Victorian art glass was a popular accent in the dining room, helping to set off and accent the silverplate. Swallows swoop across a peachblow Web vase, while an enormous Stevens and Williams cranberry glass egg is ready to delight diners as an unusual centerpiece. A cranberry glass fairy lamp also adds a colorful touch.

Values: Amber vase in stand, $750; Stevens and Williams glass egg, $2000; Cranberry glass fairy lamp, $500

A delicately painted cranberry glass watering can is a beautiful piece of Victorian art glass for any table.

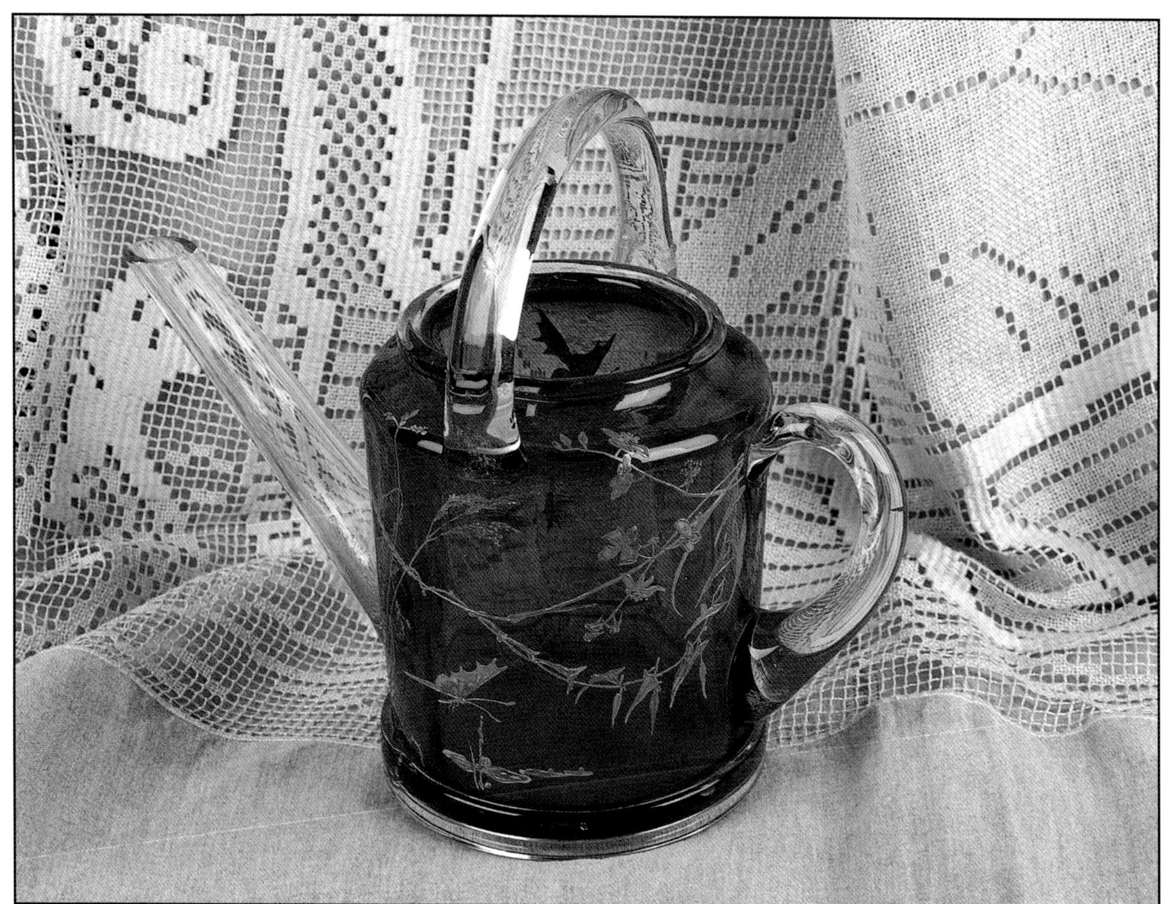

Anglo-Japanese designs were a favorite motif in the 1870s and 1880s, as seen in this biscuit barrel and relish plates in the form of Japanese fans.

Values: Cranberry glass watering pitcher, $2500; Anglo-Japanese biscuit barrel, $400; Relish plates, $250 apiece

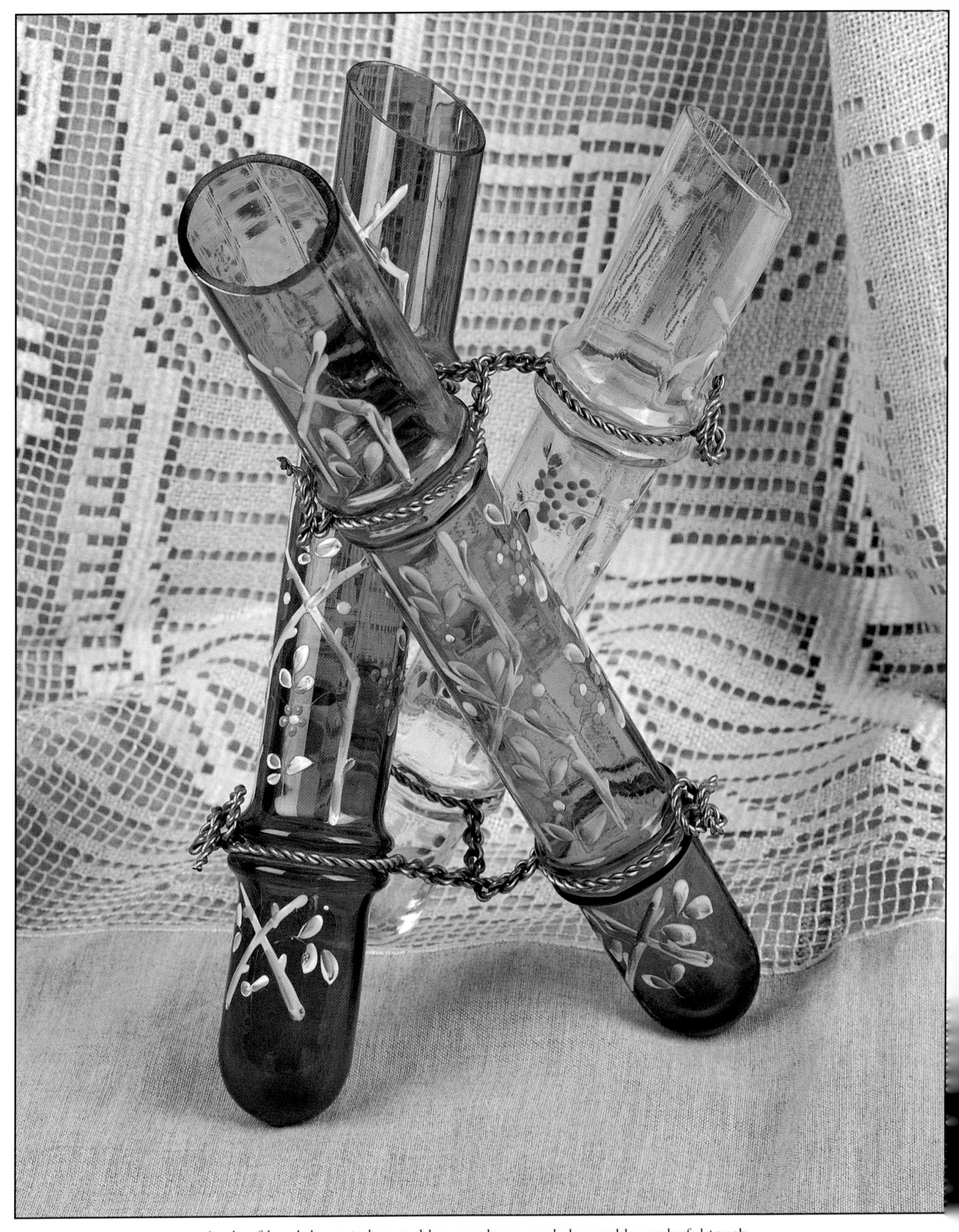

A trio of hand-decorated vases, blue, cranberry, and clear, adds a colorful touch.

Value: Decorated glass vases trio, $15

Chapter Five:

Dining Room Décor and the Table Itself

Dining rooms were considered masculine rooms in the Victorian era, decorated in deep, rich colors such as Venetian Red or Emerald Green, and often topped with a gilded and decorated ceiling. An ornate chandelier was a must, to add to the room's opulence. Furniture was heavy and often heavily carved, and set off by thick, plush portieres and drapes. The center of the room was the dining table. Victorians were not afraid to experiment with the table, perhaps layering a paisley underneath the lace tablecloth for a busier look. The table's focal point would be an ornate centerpiece, along with a pair of silver candles. Table settings were elaborate, often confusing, and some etiquette books of the period advised a befuddled diner to discreetly observe his host or hostess when uncertain as to which dining utensil was correct.

The entrance to the dining room is draped with lace and velvet portieres and guarded by an albino peacock.

Setting the Victorian dining table with a mixture of colorful glass and silverplate makes a rich and opulent look.

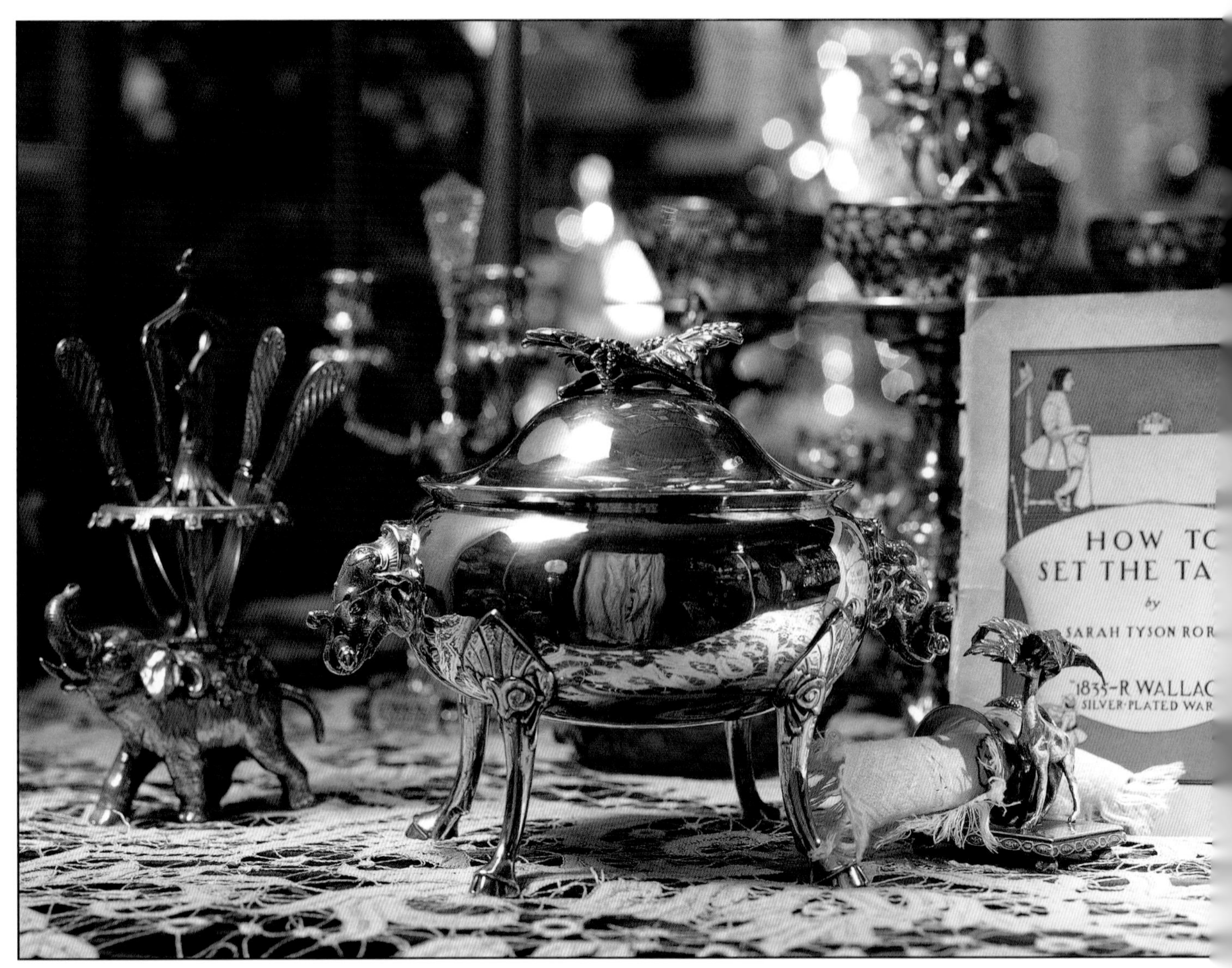

An amusing soup tureen with elephant head handles.

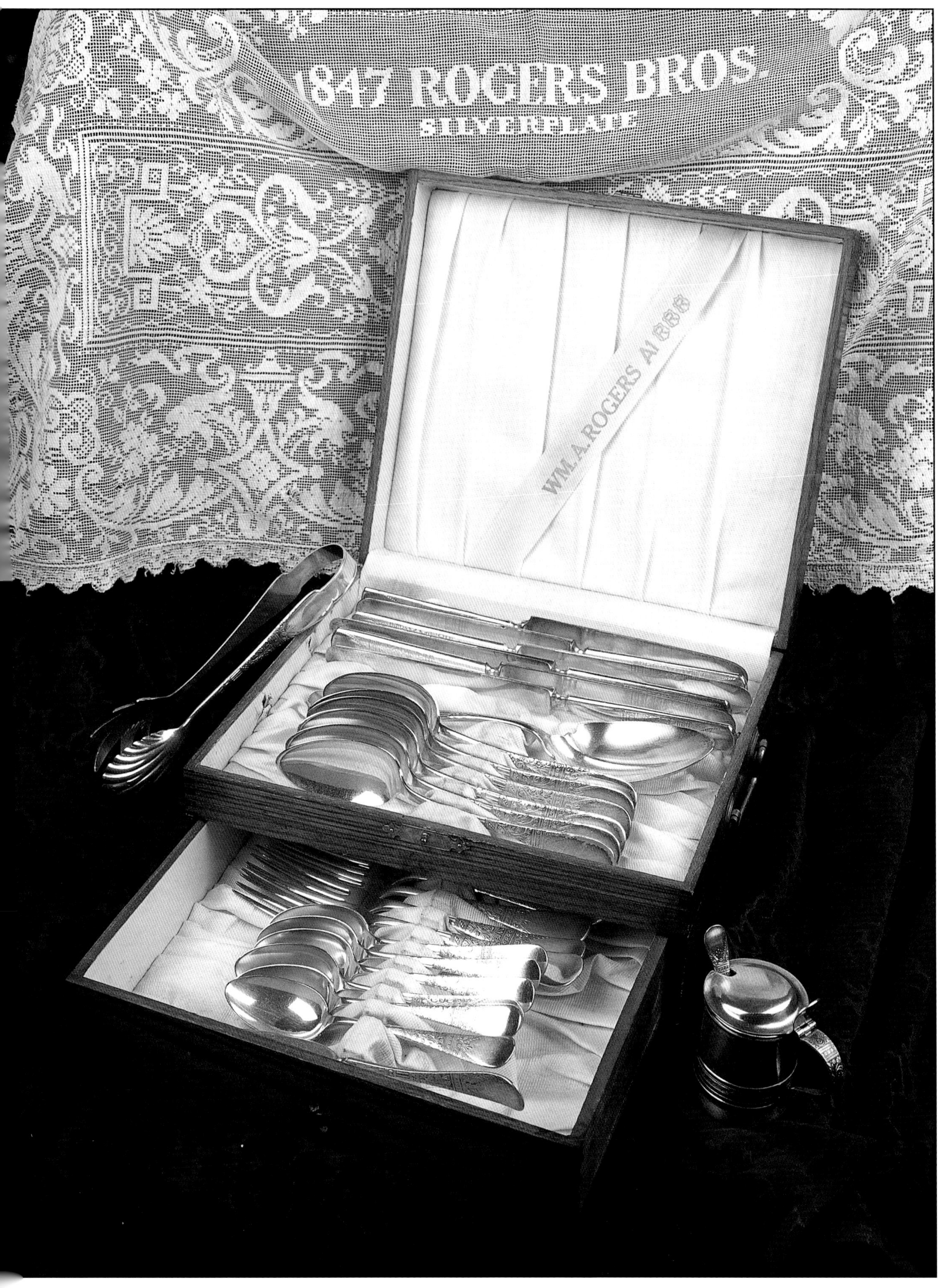

A boxed set of 1847 Rogers Brothers' Lorne pattern. The knives are especially hard to find. The individual mustard pot is also in the Lorne pattern.

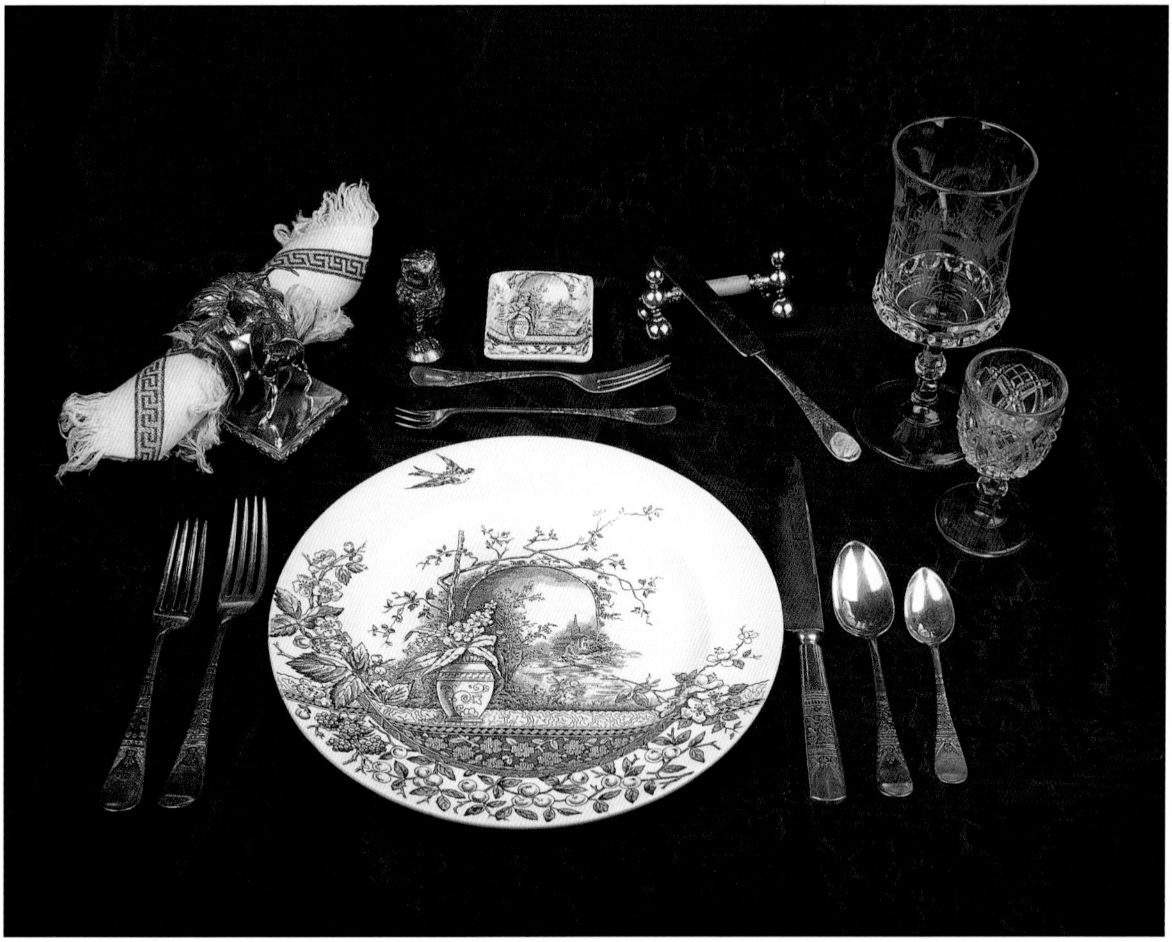

A proper, Victorian place setting included an individual knife rest, a butter pat, a fanciful napkin ring, and forks for every course, including a pastry, oyster, salad and dinner fork.

Wedgwood's Ivanhoe plates with knights and colorful Medieval figures are used along with the Gorham's Fontainebleau pattern, which also features Medieval figures, for a romantic table setting.

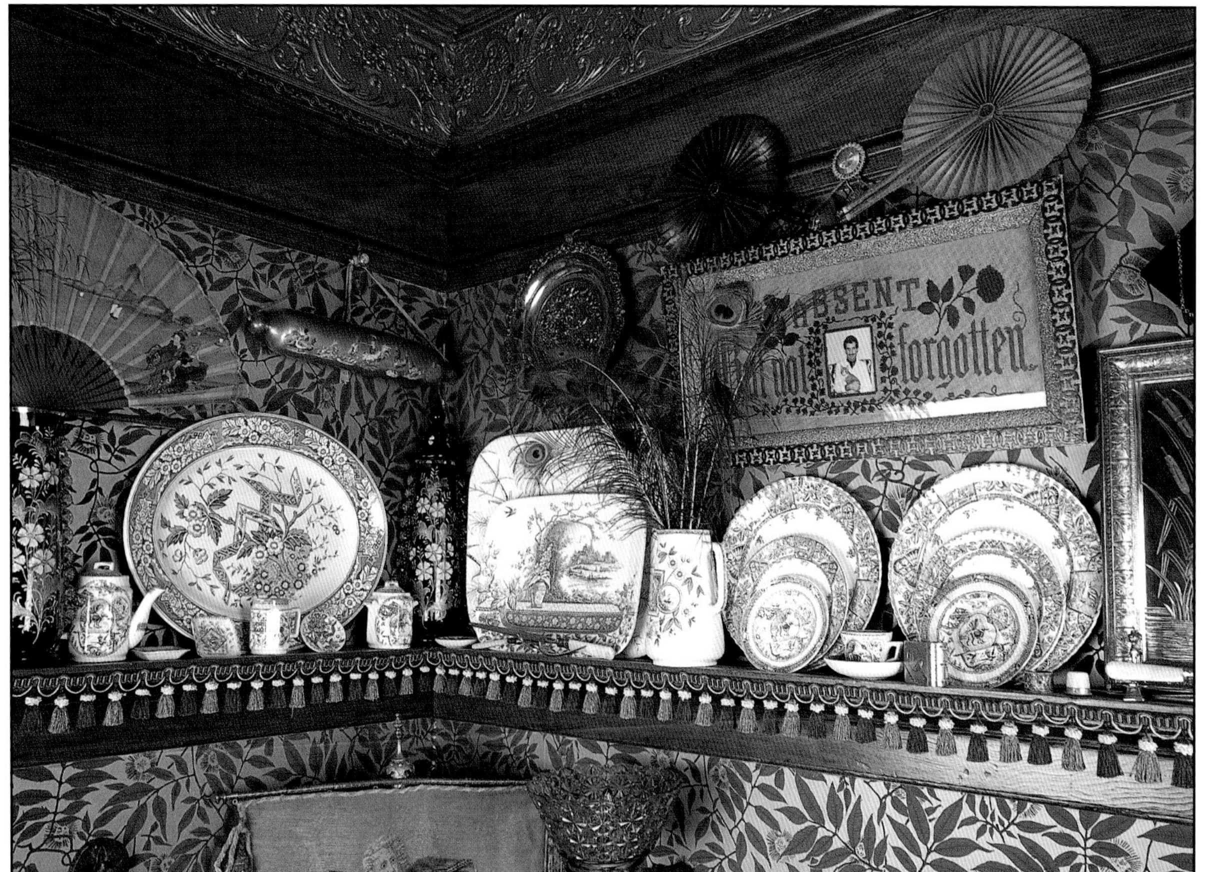

The plate rail is a good area to display part of a brown and white transferware collection.

Detail of the plate rail shows brown and white transferware among other Victoriana including this punched paper motto of "The Old Armchair," a popular song.

The plate rail displays brown and white transferware in the Burmah pattern, along with a set of Thanksgiving plates painted, of course, with turkeys.

Values, this page: Set of turkey plate
$750. Opposite page: Cranberry glas
candle guards, $500/pair

Cranberry glass candle guards are another ornament for the table. The jewel in the center of the candle guard sparkles as the candle's flame shines through it.

A napkin ring of a giraffe, resting under a palm tree, was considered a tastefully exotic accent for the Victorian table.

Values, this page: Giraffe napkin ring, $1
Opposite page: Elkington epergne, $2

An Elkington epergne, circa 1875, features an exotic Far Eastern scene of an Arab leading a camel through the palms.

Early American Pressed Glass water goblets and wine glasses make a colorful addition to the sideboard.

Values: Early American pressed glass stemware, $25 to $100 apiec

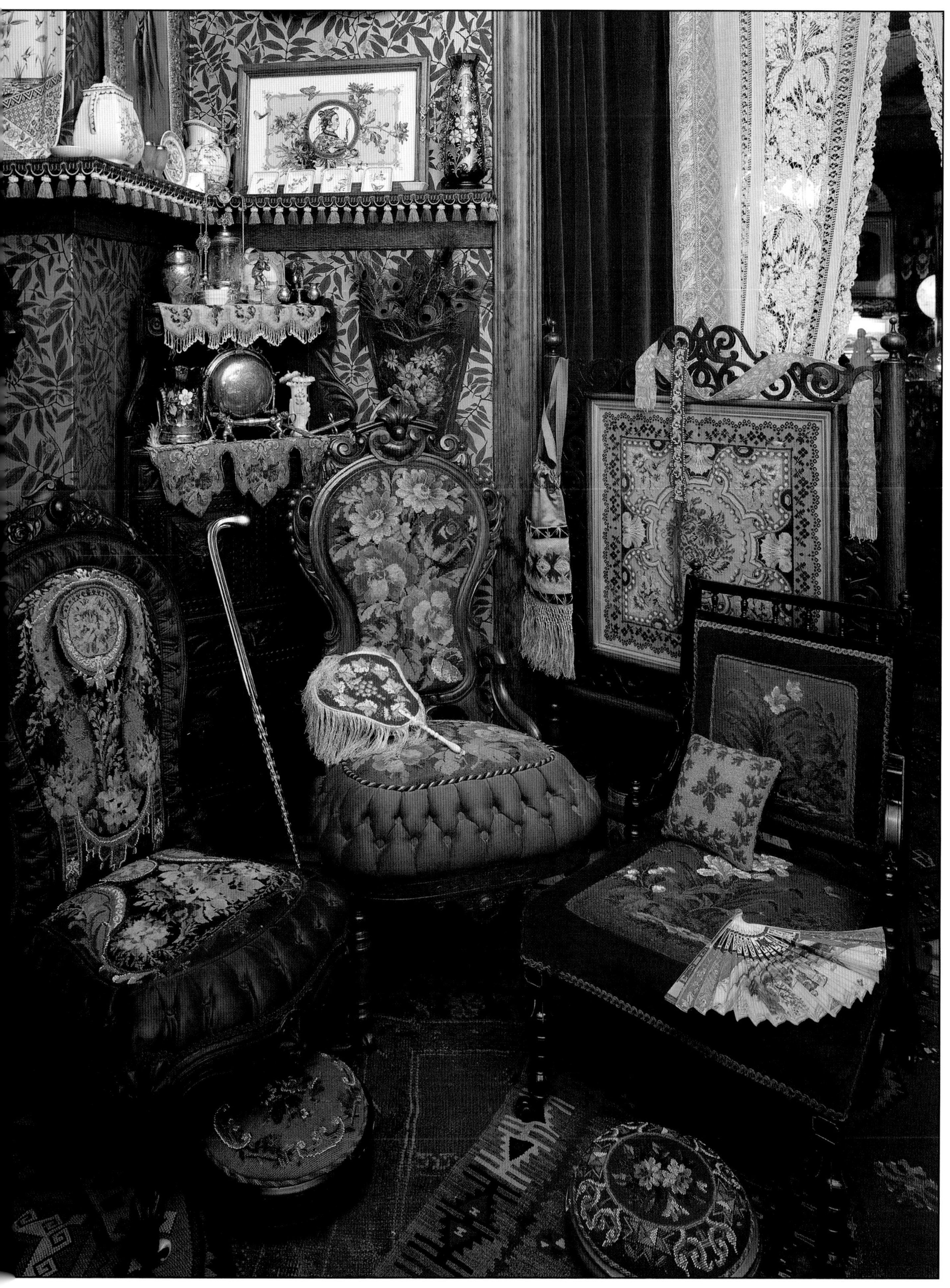

A corner of the dining room with Victorian, needlepointed chairs, footstools, and fans.

A beaded and embroidered fire screen, still on its original, brass stand, nestles in a corner beneath the plate rail that displays brown and white transferware.

Value: Beaded fire screen on brass pole stand, $17

A carved, English corner cabinet holds more silverplate and brown and white transferware.

The room's main sideboard, manufactured by the Cincinnati Art School circa 1875, is cluttered with silverplate and china.

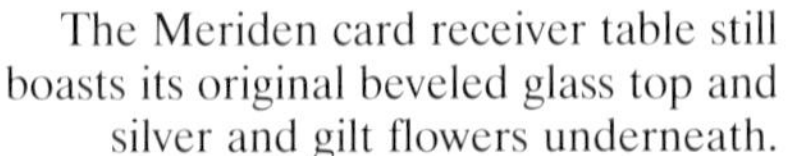

The Meriden card receiver table still boasts its original beveled glass top and silver and gilt flowers underneath.

Hands were used in every type of design, from knife rests to posy holders, in the Victorian era.

Try layering textiles for a rich and opulent look. Here the dining table is covered with a Paisley, then over layered with a delicate Battenberg lace.

Hand-embroidered, linen napkins, complete in their velvet case (also decorated with more handwork) are used to set the table.

What table setting would be complete without individual place cards, hand-decorated such as this one, held by an elegant cut-glass place card holder?

Value: Cut-glass place card holder, $250

The dining room ceiling is a richly decorated design and compliments the green and gold colors in the room.

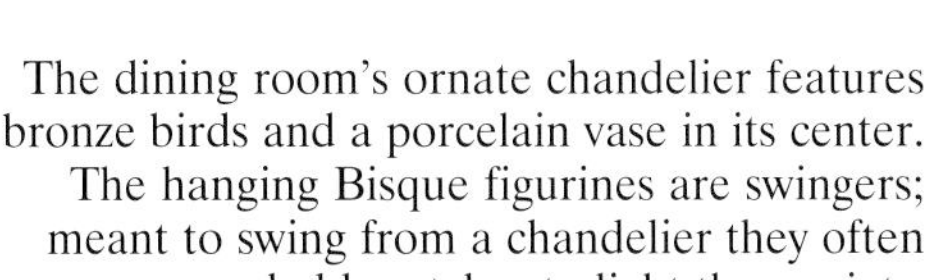

The dining room's ornate chandelier features bronze birds and a porcelain vase in its center. The hanging Bisque figurines are swingers; meant to swing from a chandelier they often held matches to light the gas jets.

ue: Bisque swingers, $250 to $750

The Barge of Venus sits in splendor amidst figural silverplate and art glass on the dining table.

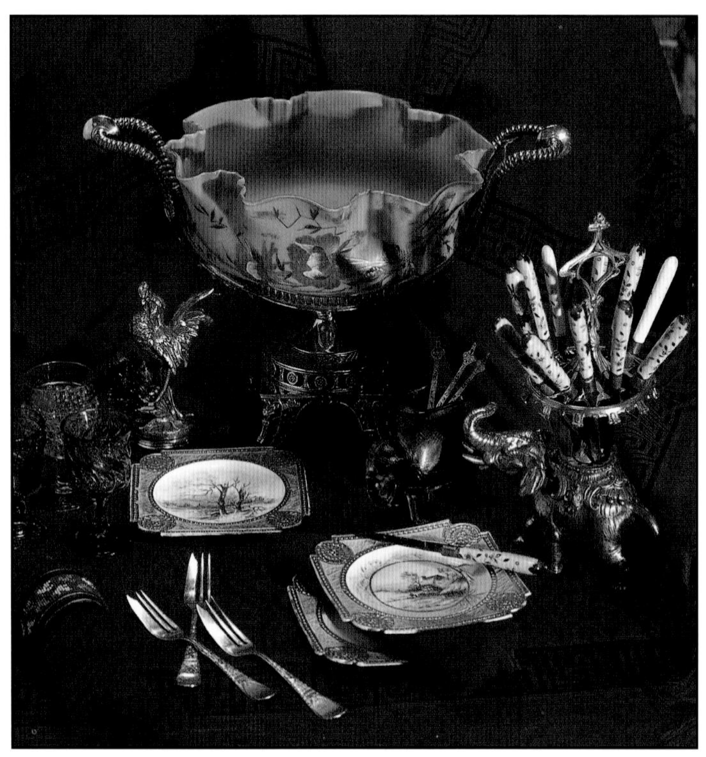

A dessert setting with china, silver, and glassware was as elaborate as the main course.

Detail of the dessert setting

Chapter Six:

Miscellaneous Oddities

The Victorian era was a time of great inventiveness and creativity, and this can be seen to full advantage in the dining room. Everything from silver-plated asparagus tongs to gold toothpicks made their appearance, and a Victorian dining room today should display at least a few of thesc curiosities to lend an appropriately creative and whimsical touch. Not to mention that Victorian oddities are great conversation pieces today, and a fun way to enliven a dinner party.

A rare, Gleason revolving castor set, circa 1850 is ready to be used on the Victorian table, along with beaded cutlery, cranberry glass, and figural silverplate.

Hand-painted small vases were popular accents for the table. They could be found both with and without elaborate silver-plated frames such as this one.

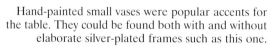

Values: Gleason revolving castor set, $5000; Hand-painted vase and stand, $300

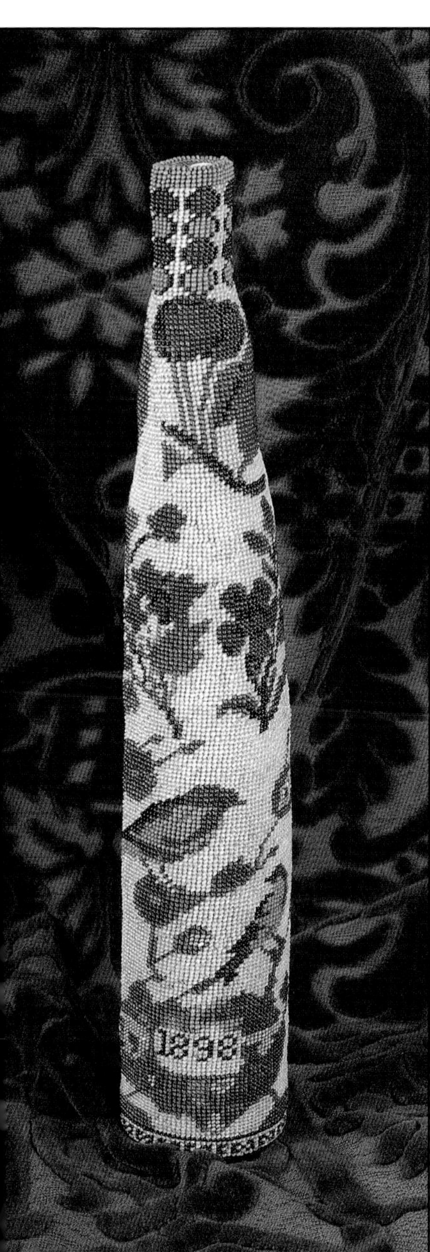

Handiwork was considered a sign of good breeding and artistic sensibility. This hand-beaded wine bottle cover, dated 1898, was made by the mistress of a Victorian home to demonstrate her needlework skills to her dinner guests.

An English swallow sails across this British Aesthetic Movement biscuit jar, circa 1885.

ue: English biscuit jar, $450

Robinson Crusoe on his little desert isle is the whimsical subject for this epergne, circa 1880, which still has its original, emerald-green glass trumpet intact.

A Mary Gregory little girl, dressed in her bonnet, holds a basket for candies or trinkets.

Values: Robinson Crusoe epergne, $350; Mary Gregory holder, $350

. silver-plated crumb set is essential to sweep the rumbs off the able between the courses.

A pair of Bradley and Hubbard candlesticks with happy frogs protected from the rain (and candle wax) by small copper umbrellas.

Values: Silver-plated crumb set, $250; Bradley and Hubbard candlesticks, $750

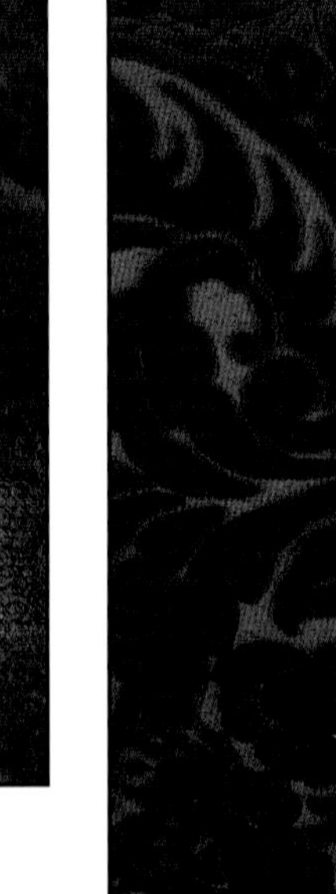

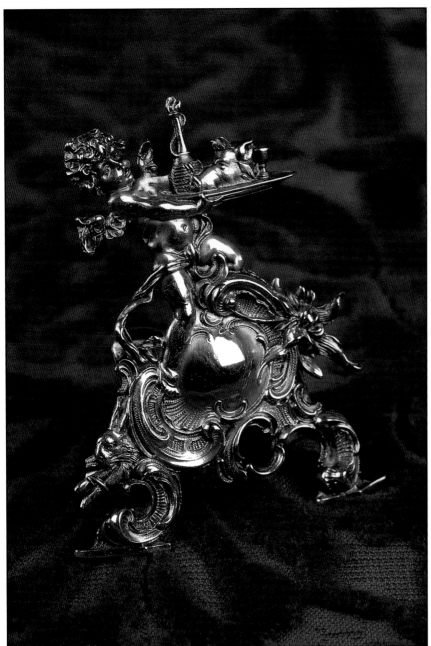

A beautifully detailed silver cherub is a charming place card holder.

A fireman's trumpet, used in Victorian ceremonial parades, makes an interesting piece of nineteenth century silverplate to add to the décor.

Values: Silver cherub place card holder, $300; Fireman's trumpet, $1750

gural toothpick
olders such as a
porcupine or a
rooster were
opular accents
for the table.

A closer look at the porcupine toothpick holder.

Value: Figural toothpick holders, $300

A match strike in the form of fly rests next t fly catcher.

Fly catchers were placed on the table and filled with sugar water to trap flies. The flies would crawl inside through the open bottom, but then were unable to fly upside down to escape.

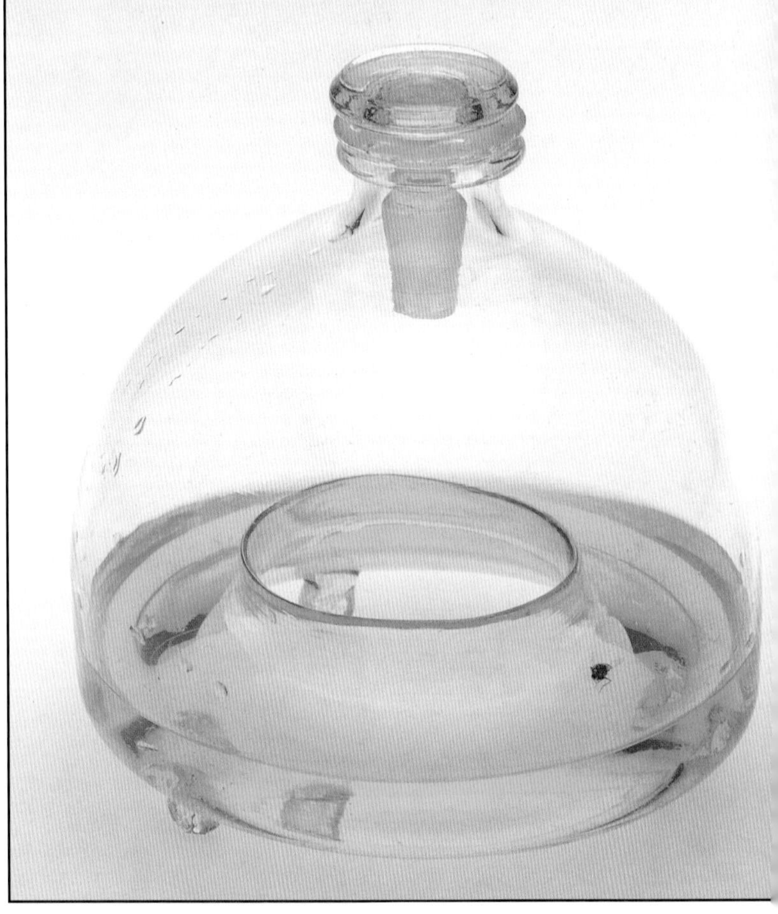

Value: Victorian glass fly catcher, $500

An orange holder, with spears to hold the orange half in place, is the perfect way to start off your breakfast.

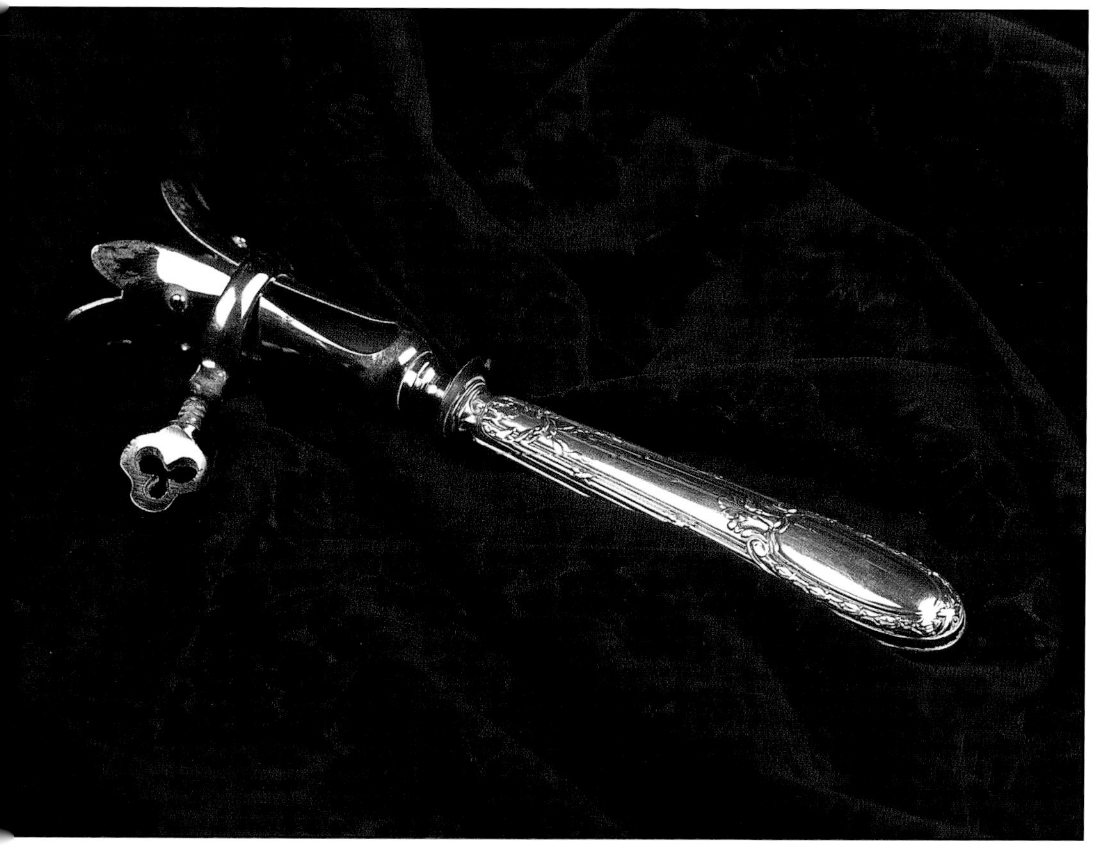

A silver-plated holder for a leg of lamb or beef, so one could carve the meat in style. The screw tightens the top, which has a circle of prongs inside to grip the leg securely.

Values: Orange holder, $300; Silver-plated meat leg holder, $300

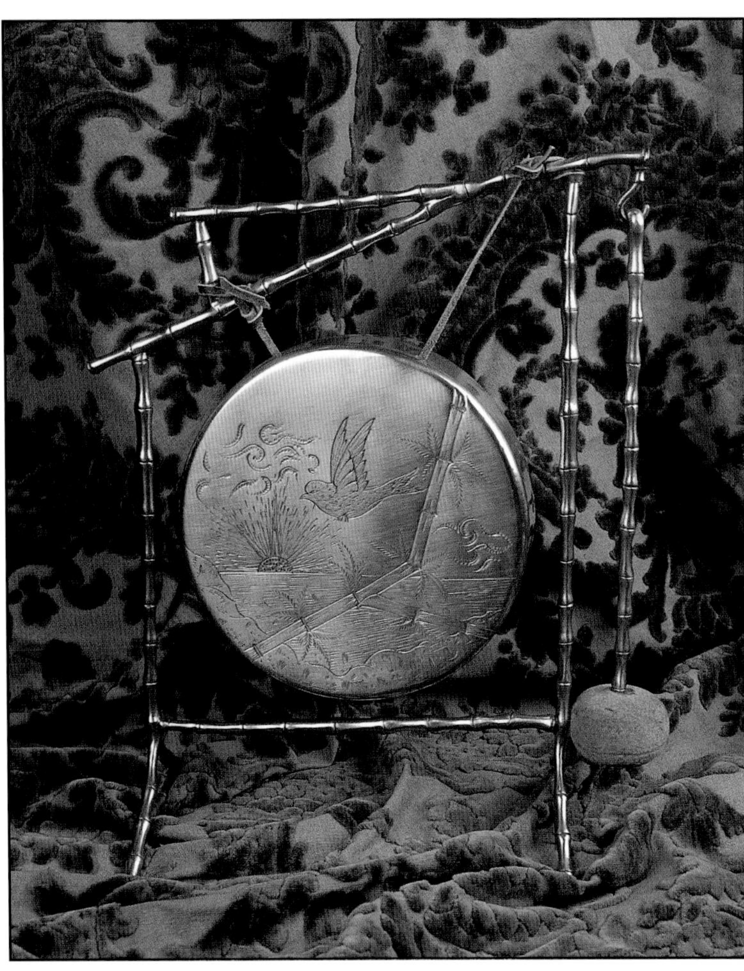

An Aesthetic Movement dinner gong summons diners in style. Circa 1880, the gong is made of copper with brass accents, featuring a swallow sailing among fields of bamboo.

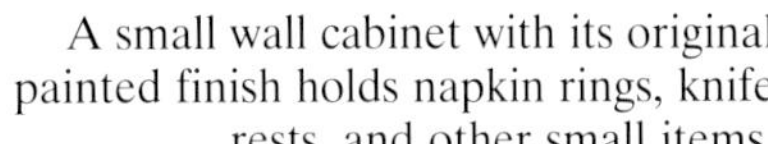

A small wall cabinet with its original painted finish holds napkin rings, knife rests, and other small items.

Value: Aesthetic copper and brass dinner gong, $800

A Puss n' Boots toothpick holder is used to hold enameled picture nails.

Figural glass pepper shakers came in a variety of forms, from Benjamin Franklin, to a rabbit, owl, elephant, and dog.

Values: Puss n' Boots toothpick holder, $500; Figural glass pepper shakers, $200 to $400

A shelf on the buffet hol
an assortment of Victori
dining items. The
lithophane plaques, at th
back, were set in front o
candle in order to view t
images.

An unusual tea caddy, in the form of a rhinoceros, has a gold-washed interior to store precious tea leaves.

Value: Rhinoceros tea caddy, $1200

Hands were popular Victorian motifs said to represent the delicate hands of Queen Victoria. Here are two spoon rests and a cigarette holder featuring hands.

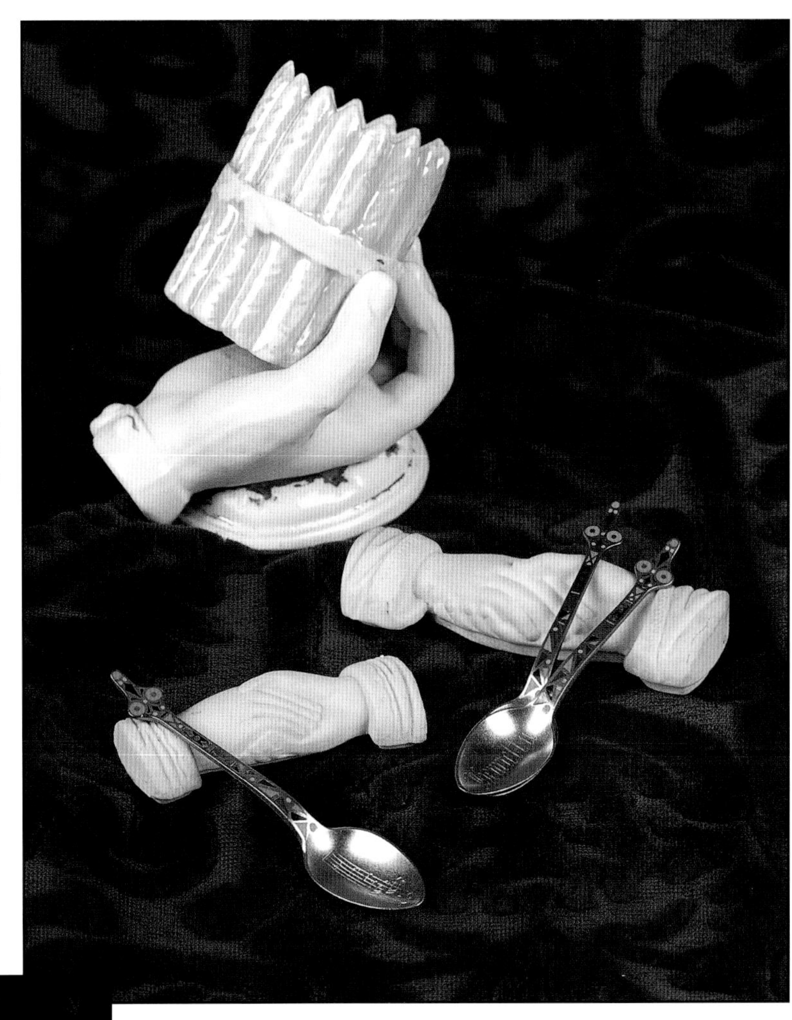

Vases also took the form of hands.

Values: Hands spoon rests, $200 apiece; Hand vases, $200 to $400

From pots to pipes, hands were popular designs.

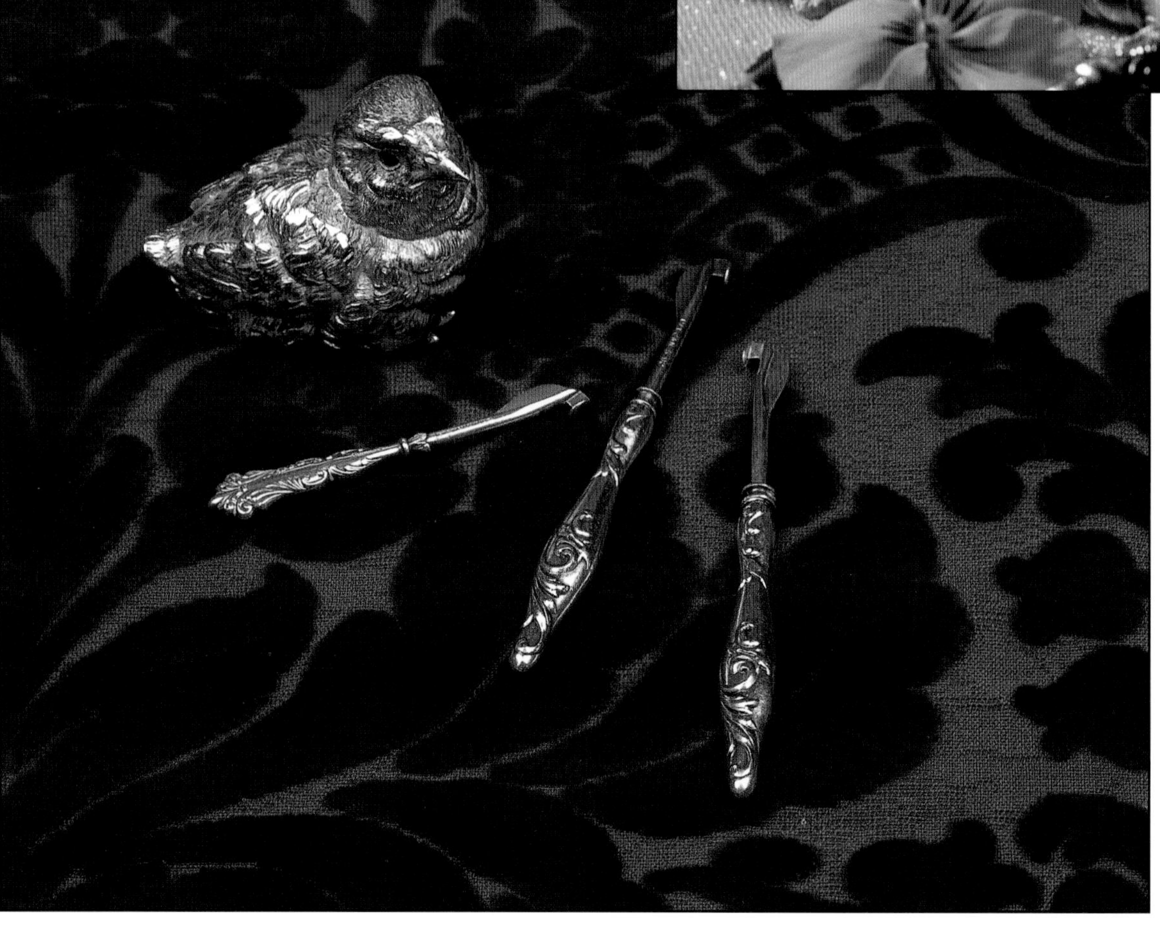

A plump robin, used as a table ornament, looks over three, rare orange slicers. The hook was used to open the orange at the navel, then the blade sliced the orange open.

Values: Orange slicers, $300; Silver robin, $250

Pepper and salt shakers were as imaginative as anything else on the Victorian dining table, as these owl pepper shakers, and cat and dog salt and pepper set show.

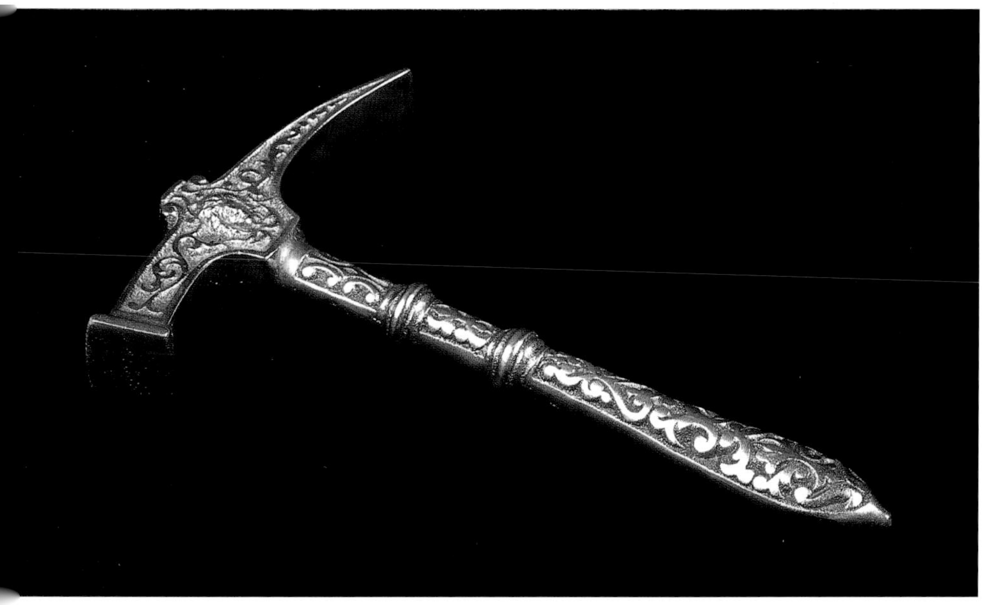

An ornate silverplate hammer used for cracking ice in style.

Values: Owl pepper shakers, $250 apiece; Cat and dog salt and pepper set, $500; Ice cracker hammer, $300

Individual condiment s
were set out for breakfa
or a simple meal.

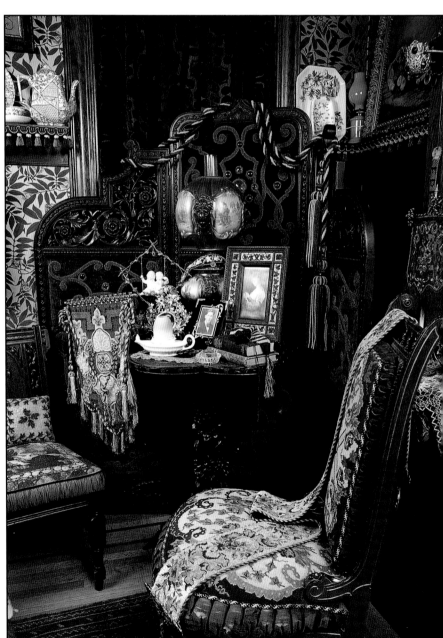

A velvet screen with faceted glass jewels creates a cozy corner and doubles as a cover for the door leading to the kitchen

Values, this page: Individual condiment sets, $300 to $500. Opposite page: 123. Cranberry honey bee, $450; Owl biscuit barrel, $500

A honey bee with a cranberry glass body and silverplate wings.

Owls were popular figures in the Victorian period, as seen in this grouping of an owl biscuit barrel and pepper shakers.

Everything from glass shoes to silverplate canoes could be found as spoon rests.

A silver-plated rack holds a pearl-handled carving set. Knives were sharpened with a silverplate knife sharpener, such as the one in front.

Values: Canoe spoon rest, $250; Glass spoon rests, $150 to $300; Silverplate carving set, $200
Knight Cruet Set, $450

lace card holders were
'ten quite elaborate, as
ese jeweled and etched
glass examples show.

Squirrels and knights are just two of the many designs made for small cruet sets meant for the breakfast table.

Values: Jeweled card holders, $150 apiece; Squirrel cruet set, $450; Knight cruet set, $450

A knight guards the goods on this breakfast, cruet set.

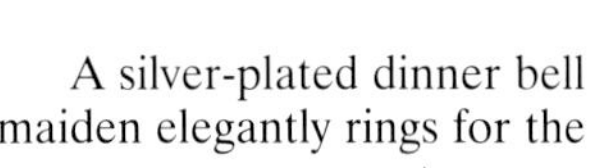

A silver-plated dinner bell maiden elegantly rings for the next course.

Value: Maiden dinner bell, $300

Smoking a cigar after a meal was a favorite Victorian ritual. The silver-plated wine bottle is actually hollow and comes apart in the center to cleverly stash the cigars. Cigar lighters came in just about every possible design, from a silver-plated, dragon-handled model to a polychromed, metallic lighter with two holders on the sides for the cigars.

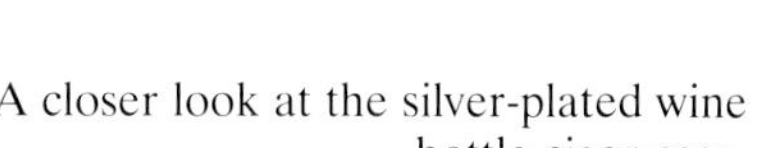

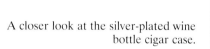

A closer look at the silver-plated wine bottle cigar case.

ue: Silver-plated bottle cigar holder, $400

A collection of beaded napkin rings adds an elegant, handmade touch to the table.

posite page: A gilded cherub holds a cranberry basket aloft for erware. A bell underneath the basket is a handy way to summon servants while you select the spoon for your next course.

Values, opposite page: Gilded cherub spooner with bell underneath, $750. This page: Beaded napkin rings, $100 to $150 apiece

Nature was a popular Victorian theme, as seen in this opalescent glass celery holder and knife rest, both adorned with butterflies.

Figural knife rests from cherubs to parrots to snails are an amusing touch to the table. One hostess likes to match each knife rest with a guest, which can make for a humorous evening.

Values: Butterfly celery holder, $500; Figural knife rests, $200 to $500 apiece

The tantalus rotates and closes the compartments for the bottles.

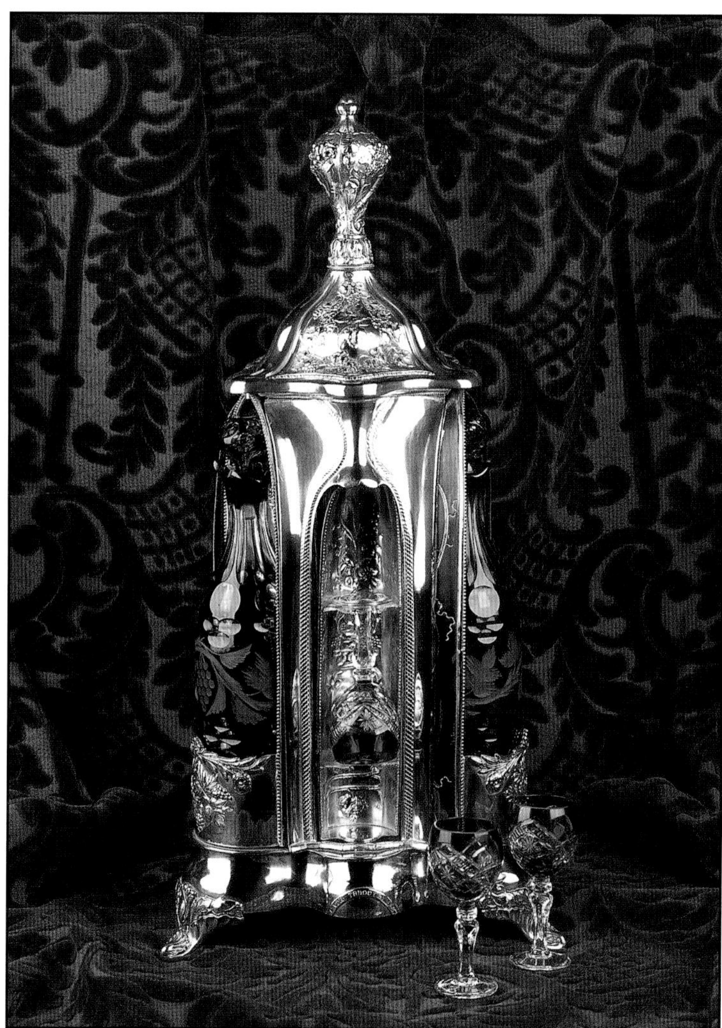

A rare Gothic, Gleason tantalus, circa 1850, still has its original, colored fruit wine bottles.

ıe: Gleason revolving tantalus, $3500

A lovely silverplate wall plaque, with its original hand-painted plate, has a butterfly on its top.

A spooner for holding spoons, vases with hands, and a Smith Brothers vase with a stork painted on the glass fill a shelf on the sideboard. The decorative enamel discs are picture nail heads.

Value: Silverplate wall plaque, $1200

The top of the buffet holds a nut bowl, place card holders, and an owl fairy lamp.

A winged nymph coyly sits atop a shell-shaped nut bowl.

Value: Winged nymph nut bowl, $1750

Toothpicks were passed out after the meal, and holders often featured whimsical animals such as this dog and rooster. Individual toothpick holders showed the good taste and breeding of their owners, as the silver and gold examples in the foreground attest.

No bowl of dry cereal for the Victorians! Breakfast came with all teh impliments, from a cooked egg warmer to an orange slicer.

Value, above photo: Figural toothpick holders, $300

Appendix

How to Set a Table

A 1901 Guide to Elegant Entertaining

The following pages are facsimile excerpts of a booklet published by The R. Wallace & Sons Mfg. Co., of Wallingford, Connecticut. Written by Mrs Sarah Tyson Rorer, it covers everything from table linens to flowers, and gives special attention to silver service, china, and glassware. Written at the close of the Victorian era, it is a capitulation of the proper way to serve a guests at your table. It covers breakfast, luncheon, dinner, tea, and supper, giving detailed instructions for the most proper way to entertain.

In addition, R. Wallace included several patterns of its "1835-R. Wallace" Silver-plated Ware at the back of the booklet. These are informative in showing the great variety of forms that were available, and in naming their various functions.

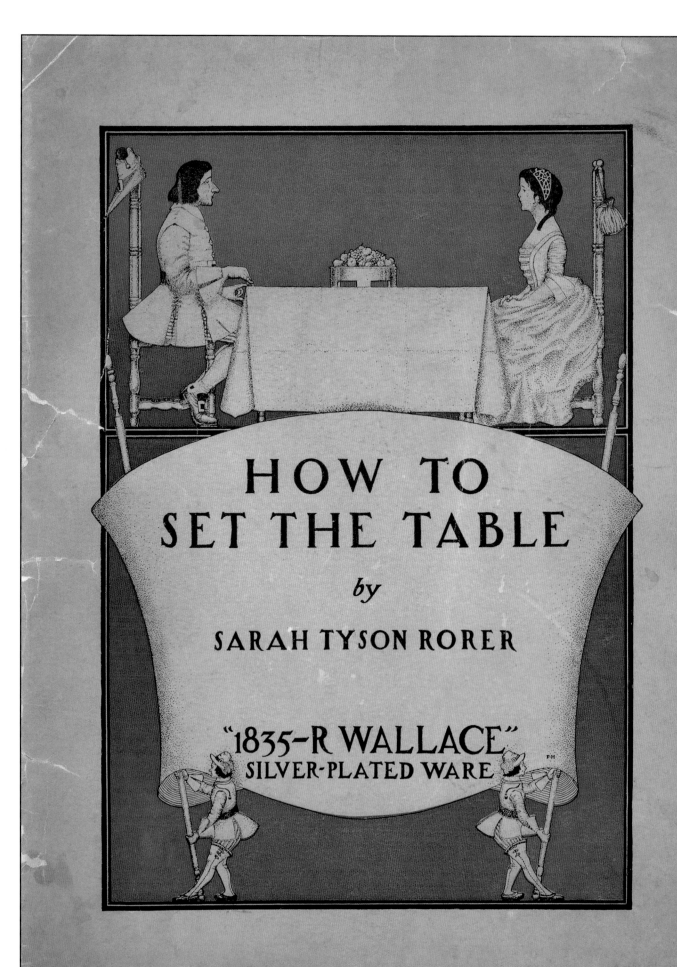

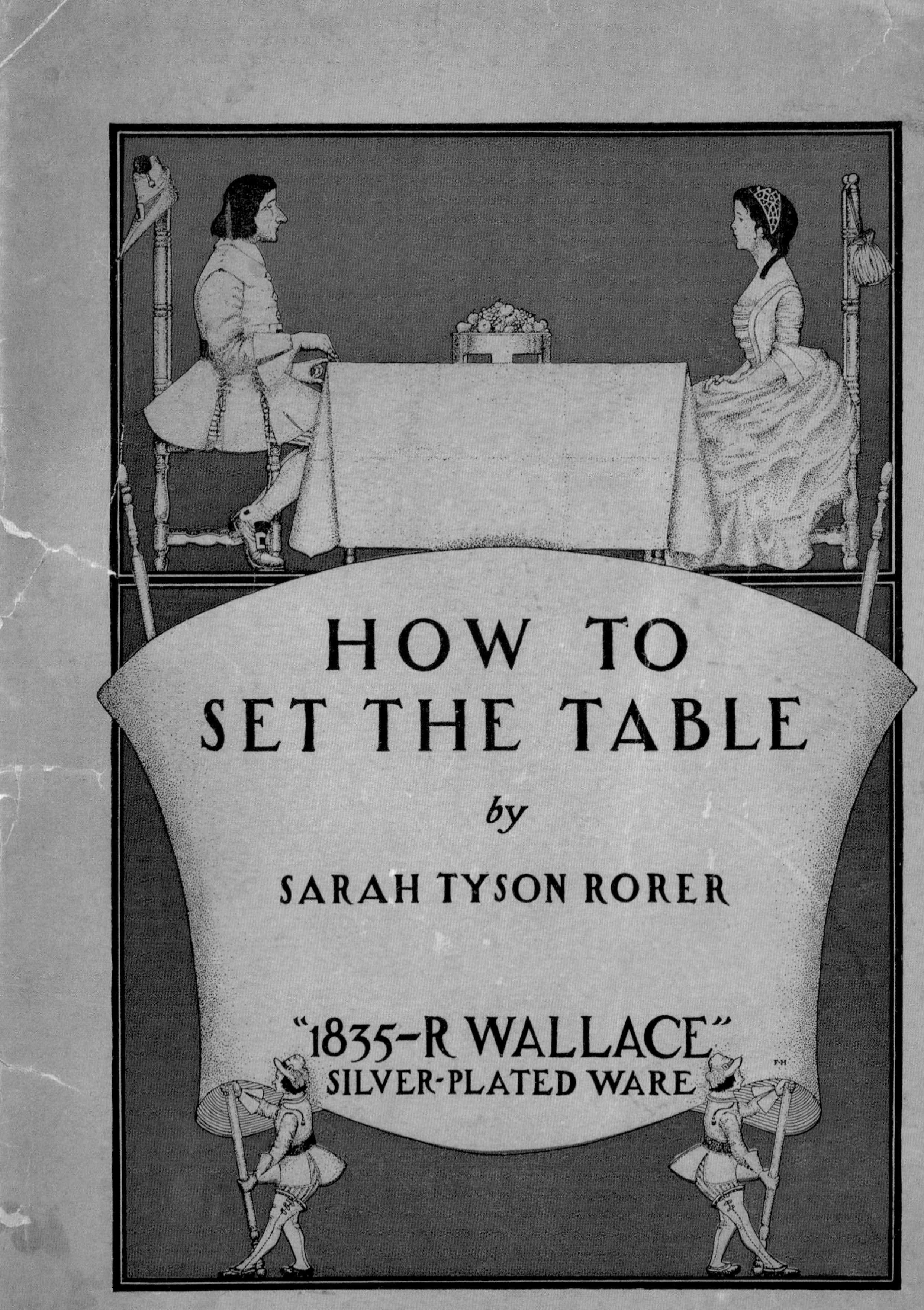
HOW TO
SET THE TABLE
by
SARAH TYSON RORER
"1835-R WALLACE"
SILVER-PLATED WARE

HOW TO SET THE TABLE

How to Set the Table

Being a Treatise upon this Important Subject by

MRS. SARAH TYSON RORER

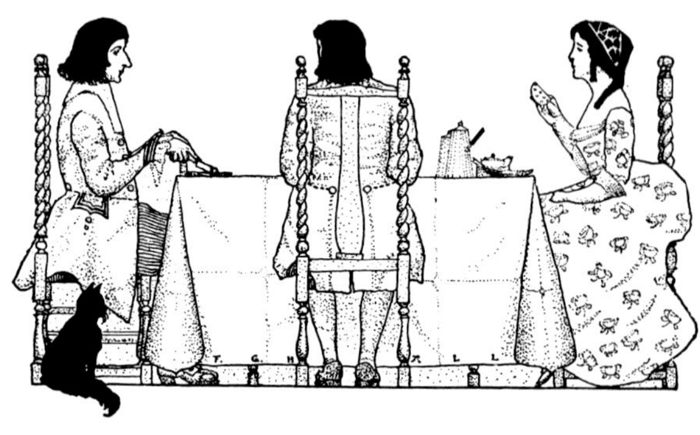

Published by R. WALLACE & SONS MFG. CO.

MAKERS OF THE FAMOUS

"1835–R. WALLACE" SILVER PLATED WARE

WALLINGFORD, CONNECTICUT

NEW YORK · CHICAGO · SAN FRANCISCO · LONDON

Designed & Printed by
The University Press
Cambridge, U. S. A.

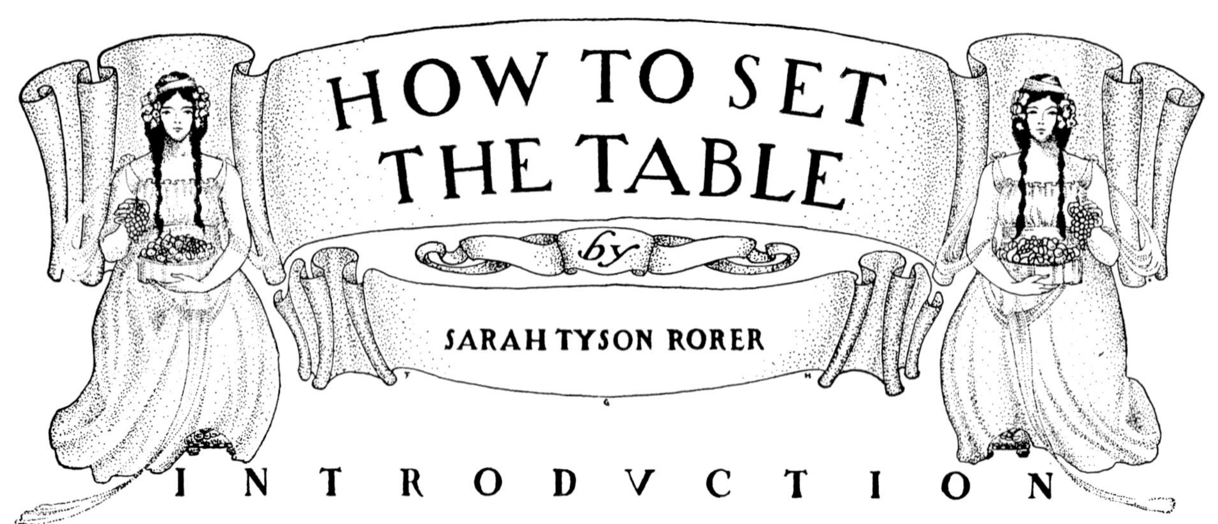

SERVICE at table demands absolutely spotless linen, carefully laundered and plainly folded. There are of course fashions in linens as in other things, but the laws governing them are sufficiently flexible to accommodate themselves to the purse of people of moderate means.

Do not place the cloth on the table's bare wooden top; lay first a blanket or padding made for the purpose. It deadens the sound and gives the linen a firmer and better appearance. Do not starch either tablecloths or napkins. They must hang in soft, smooth folds from the edge of the table. Knives and forks to be handsome should be of medium size, and, if the purse permits, have sets for each course. It is also necessary to have two, better three, carving sets, two large and one small. The largest one will be used for roasts and turkey; the second size for fowls; the smallest for steaks and birds. We have, in these days, many special pieces of silver, dainty and convenient, as butter picks, cheese knives, asparagus tongs, cake knives, pie and ice cream servers, Saratoga chip servers, jelly spoons, cold meat forks, and salad sets.

BREAKFAST

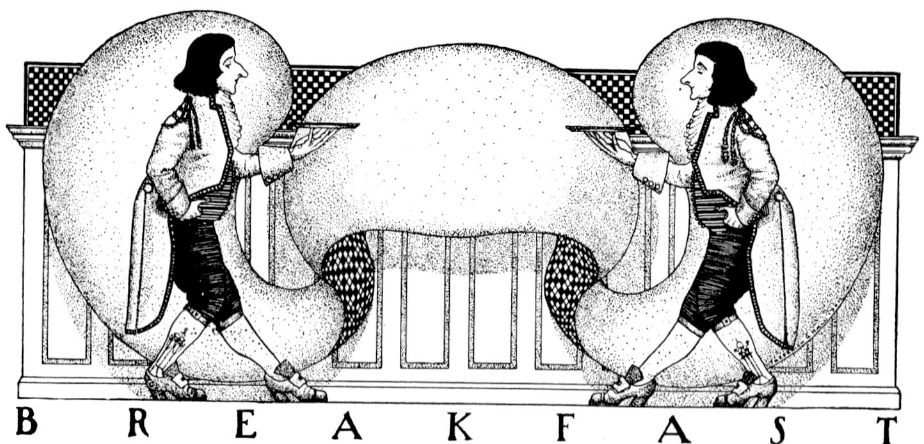

B R E A K F A S T

A COMPANY breakfast and a luncheon are about the same. Here you may use a cloth or a bare table; the latter is preferable providing the table is well polished. A few flowers or a fern stand may be placed on the mirror in the centre, a rack of toast on one side, a tray of rolls on the other. At each place a plate holding a fruit doily; a finger bowl just on the left, a meat fork, and the breakfast napkin. On the right a plain knife, dessert spoon for the cereal, egg spoon, and orange spoon. Back of the finger bowl, on a fruit plate, a fruit knife. At the head, to the left, bread and butter plate with butter spreader, to the right the water glasses; between these the individual salt cellars with individual salt spoons.

In front of the hostess place a neatly arranged dish of fruit. In front of the host, a hot-water covered dish containing the cereal, or, if cereal is not used, scrambled eggs. Fruit is usually served first, then cereal, then meat or eggs and coffee.

If flowers are not accessible or fern stand not at hand, place the fruit in the centre of the table.

The complete breakfast service consists of fruit basket or dish, individual fruit plates, knives or spoons, finger bowls and fruit doilies, or a berry bowl, individual berry saucers with berry forks, or a melon

tray and silver individual melon plates with fruit knife and fruit fork, porridge or cereal dish, and individual porridge bowls; bread tray, toast rack, hot-water dish, a silver covered meat dish or chop plate, individual breakfast plates, bread and butter dishes, butter spreader, coffee service with coffee cups and saucers; covered silver vegetable dish for such things as creamed potatoes, egg tray or boiler, egg cups and egg spoons, a carafe with ordinary tumblers, a chocolate pot, chocolate muddler, individual cups and chocolate spoons. Where hot cakes are served, a covered cake dish, with large, flat, silver hot cake server, individual plates, and pastry forks are used. A pastry fork has one tine in the form of a blade. Large butter dish with cover and butter knife is used for breakfast. If, however, the butter is made into balls, serve with butter pick.

LVNCHEON

LVNCHEON

LVNCHEON

L V N C H E O N

A LUNCHEON is served after the manner of a dinner; a bare table or tablecloth may be used. Either would be quite proper. The service will consist of fern stand, bouillon cups, chop tray, casserole or round covered dish, large vegetable dish, silver sandwich tray, chocolate and coffee and tea service, plates smaller than dinner plates, salad bowl with the necessary silver and individual plates, celery or olive tray and spoon, bread and butter plates and butter spreaders, fruit basket or comport, with individual fruit plates, ice cream set with knife and spoon for helping, and individual ice cream forks and spoon, water and Apollinaris glasses, a small china tub for cracked ice, ice tongs, and such extra pieces as jelly knives, cake knives, Saratoga chip servers, and asparagus tongs. After arranging the fern stand, place around in graceful manner small dishes containing olives, celery, and bonbons; individual salts may be used or not as one prefers. At the right of the individual plates arrange the knives, blades turned in and to the left the forks. At the head of the plate, to the right, stand the glasses, at the left the bread and butter plates with the spreaders placed carelessly on the plates; the napkins to the extreme

left — a roll or bit of bread may be placed in the fold. If bouillon is to be served first, the cups may be filled and placed just as luncheon is announced. The next service, an *entrée*, as patties, may be served from the side on hot plates. The serving will be continued the same as for a dinner. If chocolate is served for lunch it may be placed with the dessert course, or right after the salad, if it is to be used as dessert. If cake forms a portion of the dessert, pass the loaf, allowing each to cut a piece to suit the individual taste.

In the illustrations a choice is given with bare table or with cloth. With the cloth you have the first service (bouillon) placed just as luncheon is announced. Arrangement on bare table would be precisely the same.

On the bare table you have salad service with dressing in a boat, and the chocolate service just placed. Wafer or toast served from a sideboard or side table. With the salad course the bread and butter plates are frequently allowed to remain. Chocolate is poured just as the salad plates are being removed.

On the second bare table we have an ice cream service with loaf cake. It is always wise to put both cake knife and fork on the plate before it is passed.

DINNER

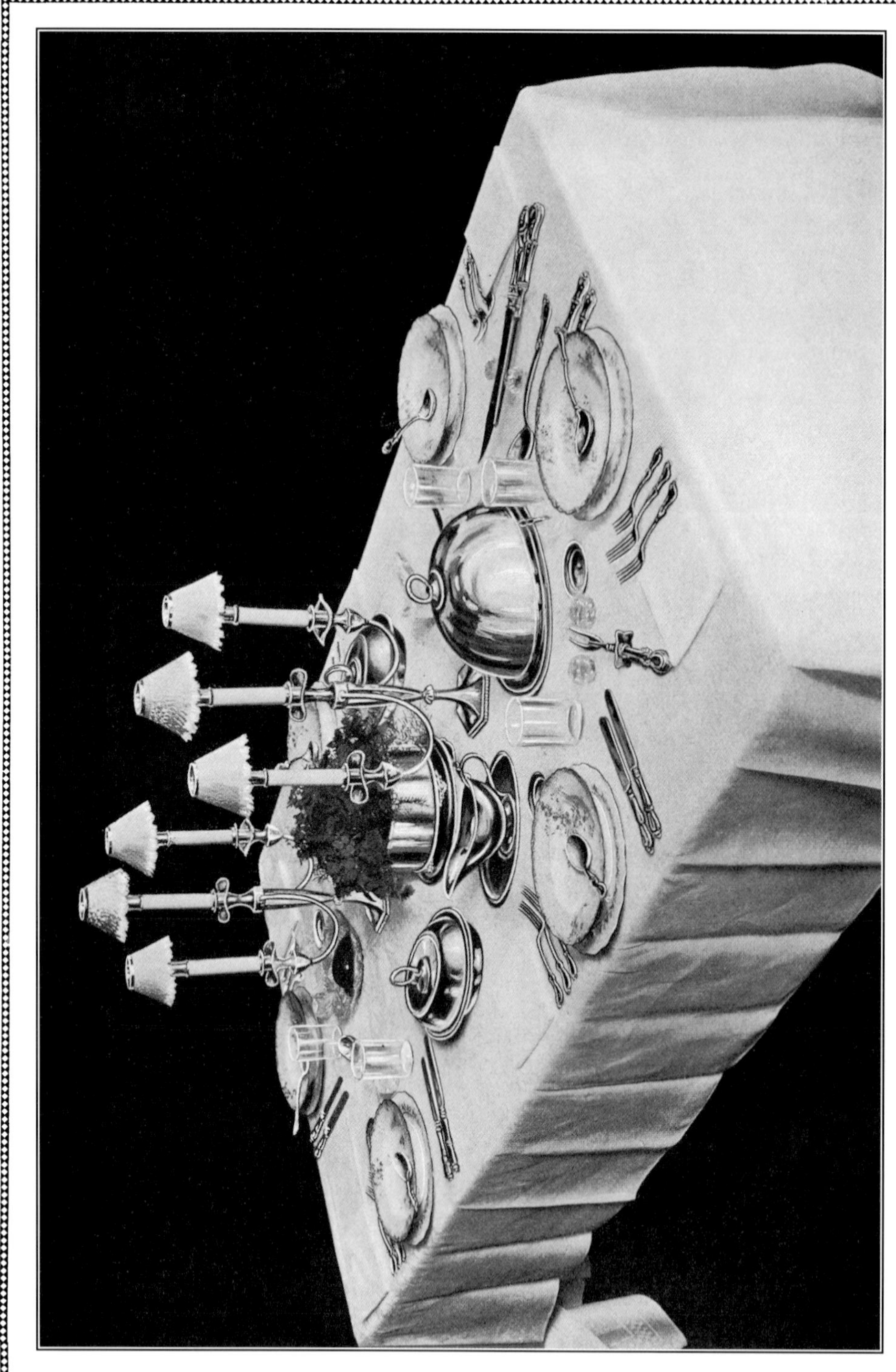

DINNER

DINNER

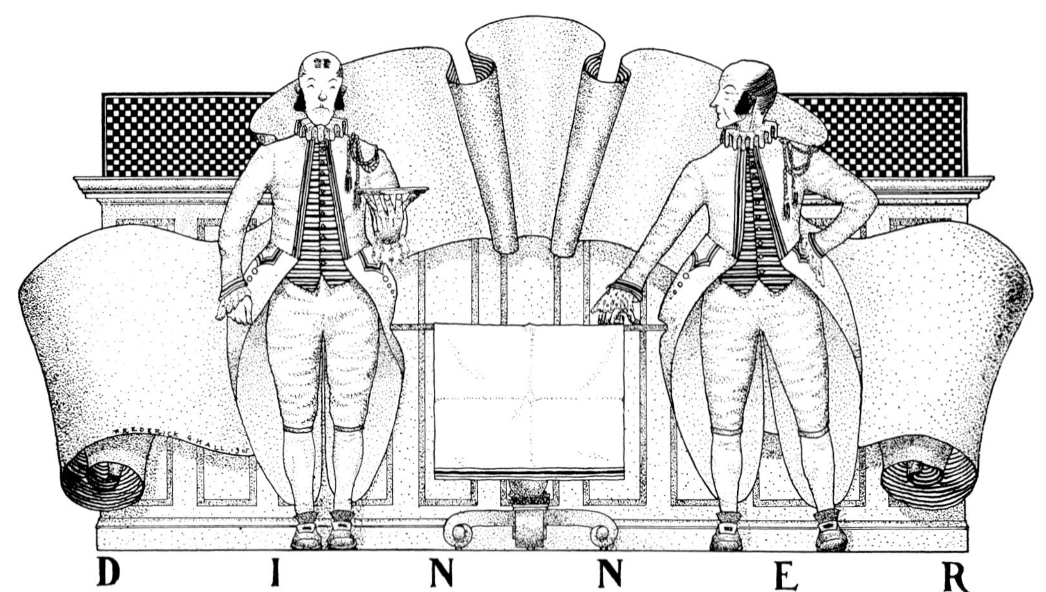

D I N N E R

A DINNER may consist of from five to ten courses, and is served from five to seven or eight o'clock. No matter how many courses, each must be served quickly and quietly, without apparent haste. The success of dinner depends much upon the setting and decoration of the table. After the tablecloth is spread place in the centre either a large flower vase or fern stand; if the former, select flowers free from heavy odor, and to correspond with the lighting and coloring of the dining-room. Olives, radishes, and celery are now placed on the table. Arrange them in neat cut glass or silver dishes and add sufficient cracked ice to keep them cool. Do not serve celery in a high glass stand. Put at the head of each plate an individual salt cellar; on top of this place an individual salt spoon. Place the napkins to the left, knives on the right hand side, blades turned in. Nearest the plate the dessert knife, next the meat knife, still to the right the fish knife, then soup spoon, and on the outside, to the right, the oyster fork. On the left, nearest the plate, dessert fork, next salad, next meat, and on the outside the fish fork. The service will be used from the outside toward the plate. Butter is not,

as a rule, served at dinner; so butter chips or plates are not used. On the right, at the head of the knives, place a tumbler for water and the wineglasses. At the head of the table, in front of the host, place the carving knife and fork, and steel.

Oysters and clams on half shell are served first. Fill luncheon or breakfast plates with finely cracked ice, sink the deep shell down into it, stand these in a dinner plate, and place them just as dinner is announced. In removing these plates for the soup course the dinner plates will remain. The soup service consists of soup tureen and individual soup plates. The tureen will be placed in front of the hostess; each plate as helped is placed in the dinner plates on the table. The next, the fish course, gives the hostess a fine opportunity to display her artistic taste in china. The service is a large fish dish, a sauce boat, a platter and a ladle, and individual plates. The dinner plates and soup plates will now be removed, and hot fish plates brought in. In a small dinner the roast comes next, and is served on large carefully heated dinner plates. The vegetables are brought in on silver or china dishes and placed on the table and passed after the meat is served. This, being the main course, demands the most elaborate of the dinner service. Next in order is the salad. A plain salad should be dressed by the hostess, passed by the waiter, allowing each one to help one's self. Use a long lettuce fork for tearing the lettuce; then place at the side of the dressed salad a salad fork and spoon for serving. After this everything is removed from the table but the last wineglasses, the water tumblers and the mineral water tumblers, and dessert knives and forks. The olives and salted almonds may also be removed if you wish. The table is crumbed, ice cream and cake are brought in. The ice cream service consists of ice cream knife and ladle for helping. Have deep dessert plates, ice cream forks and spoon, and, if berries are to be served, a berry fork. If the cake is large and served whole, put a cake knife on the side of the plate.

This knife has a saw at the back for sawing through the icing, which prevents the crumbling and cracking. If coffee is to be served at the table with crackers and cheese, finger bowls and small plates with cheese knives will now be brought in. The after-dinner service and tray will be placed in front of the hostess.

Where asparagus is served as a salad, the service will consist of silver asparagus platter (a dish with drainer in the bottom) and boat in small platter, on the side of which you place a small ladle, asparagus tongs, and individual salad plates. Salad always follows the meat course, unless there is game, in which case it will be served with the game. When a mayonnaise dressing is served, the mayonnaise will be brought in in a small boat on platter, using the small ladle in serving. If pudding is used in the place of ice cream, serve on a large round pudding dish, with large gravy boat with ladle to correspond. The service will consist of small pudding dishes, which, by the way, are small soup dishes. If the pudding is a hot one, slip the inside dish into a silver covering. This protects the table, and hides any spots on the dish which may have occurred in the baking. Where a soft cream cheese is used, place it on a flat dish, and serve with a cheese knife. Edam or pineapple will be served in a silver holder with a cheese scoop.

A full dinner service in silver consists of silver soup tureen, large meat platter with cover, two vegetable dishes (silver), the tops of which have movable handles, allowing them to be used also as dishes; a silver fish platter, four sets of knives, fruit, dessert, fish, and meat; six sets of forks, oyster, fish, meat, salad, game, and dessert; soup, ice cream, and dessert spoons; a large and a small carving set; a long gravy spoon, gravy boat, platter, and ladle, small boat with small ladle for a salad dressing, individual salt spoons, mustard and horse-radish spoon, and extra silver, as jelly knife, asparagus tongs, ice tongs, salad fork and spoon, cake knife and fork, small sugar tongs, and the black coffee service, consisting of three pieces, a pot, sugar, and cream jug, with of course small individual spoons.

A Word About the Selection of Table Glass

Goblets are preferable to tumblers. Sauterne decanters have handles, the glasses with graceful tops, the bowls light green, the stems crystal. Madeira decanters have large bowls, no handles. Sherry glasses are simply slightly flaring at the top. The decanters and glasses used for Rhine wine have very tall stems, and are usually richly gilded. Sherbet cups are the same as lemonade glasses, small with handles. Champagne is best served from the original bottle into saucer-shaped glasses with hollow stems, although a small flaring tumbler is preferred by many. Hock and Burgundy wines, as well as claret, are served in plain crystal glasses, a size between the sherry and sauterne. Many prefer claret in a tumbler, that water may be added. Port decanters and glasses are smaller than those used for claret, and are without handles; plain white crystal is to be preferred. A regular claret set consists of two decanters, without handles, glasses are like low small goblets in plain crystal. Claret should never be served in colored glasses. For cognac, select small, white cut glass decanters without handles, and very small glasses. Tiny thimble-shaped glasses are used for serving liqueurs; the decanters are very small and without handles. These may be plain or colored. A punch bowl and large ladle are often the pride of the hostess, and may be either china, richly ornamented, or cut glass. For claret cup use a tall cut glass pitcher with a silver binding at the top, a claret ladle for serving. This ladle has a long, straight handle. A punch bowl ladle is larger in size, but shaped more like a soup ladle. Iced tea or coffee glasses are light and tall, and should hold nearly one pint. An iced tea spoon has a long handle and round bowl. Water carafes are made in plain French or cut glass. Mineral water glasses are light, thin, straight, and plain, usually sold under the name of Apollinaris glasses.

FIVE O'CLOCK TEA

HIS is at best a very light repast, and consists of tea or chocolate with wafers or small cakes, or a glass of sherbet and wafers. The table should be daintily laid with china, delicate in design and texture, cups and saucers odd, and five o'clock tea spoons. The water kettle may be of copper, brass, or silver, and should be in good condition and highly polished. Sandwiches and thin wafers are arranged on dainty china plates, simply passed as the tea or chocolate is poured. A silver tea ball is a great convenience, as it enables one to easily lift the tea ground from the infusion, so that in standing the tea does not become bitter. If chocolate is served it may be made outside and brought to the table in a serving pot.

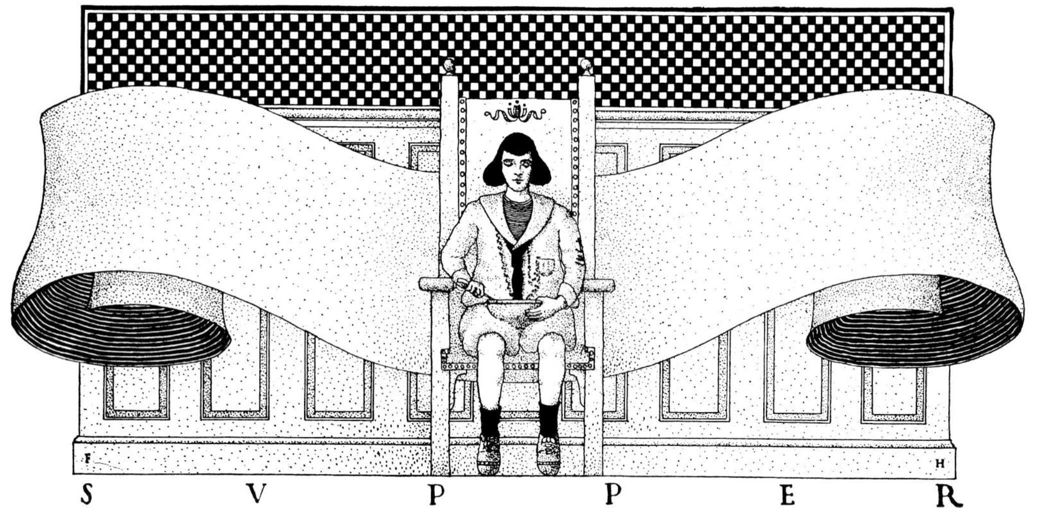

AT supper the service is placed on the table at the beginning. A large coffee tray covered with a tray linen or tray cloth is placed at the foot of the table. On this the entire service, consisting of tea and water pot, sugar and cream jugs and bowl. At the head of the table on one side place the butter, on the other the cake with knife and fork, and directly in front the salad or cold meat. For a salad use a salad fork and spoon for serving; for meat, cold meat fork. A dish of jelly with jelly spoon or knife. Serve cooked fruit with large fruit spoon. In the centre, instead of flowers, use a comport of fruit. At the right of the individual plates place a small knife, a dessert knife, and then a teaspoon. On the left a dessert fork, a small meat fork, and sardine fork.

A full supper service consists of silver tea set, tea plates, bread tray, cold meat dish, silver covered hot water dish for such things as creamed sweetbreads, fruit dish, china or cut glass, teacups and saucers, berry sets with berry saucer and forks, water tumblers, and chafing dish. A chafing dish is a great convenience.

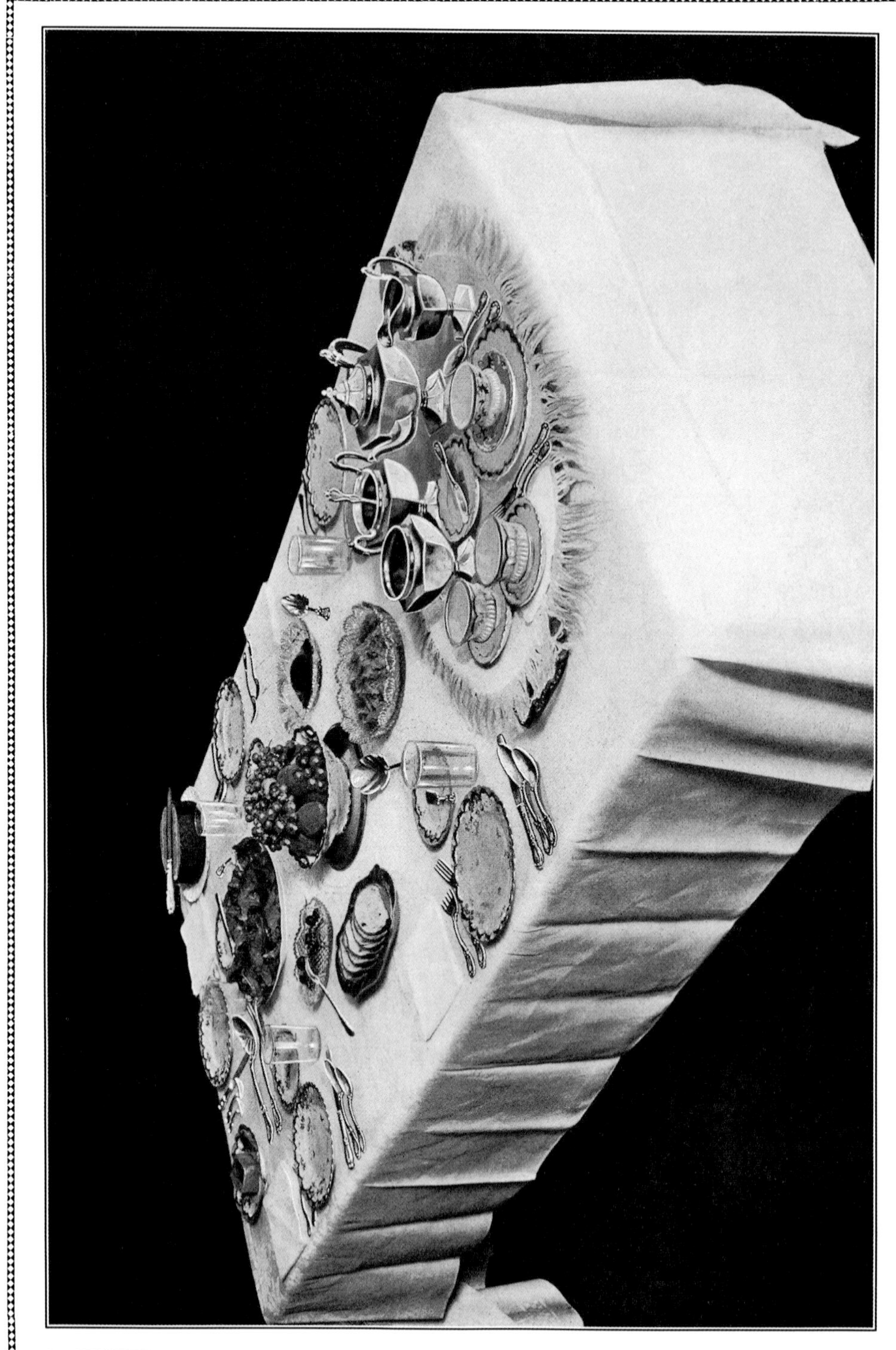

SVPPER

Trade Mark
"1835-R. WALLACE"

The "Astoria" Pattern

Cuts one-third actual size

1 Medium Fork 2 Olive Fork 3 Berry Fork 4 Small Cold Meat Fork 5 Smoked Beef Fork	6 Individual Salad Fork 7 Sardine Fork 8 Ice Cream Fork 9 Child's Fork 10 Child's Knife	11 Child's Spoon 12 Oyster Fork 13 Dessert Fork 14 Cold Meat Fork 15 Pickle Fork	16 Asparagus Fork 17 Lettuce Fork 18 Cake Fork

34

Trade Mark
"1835-R. WALLACE"

The "Astoria" Pattern

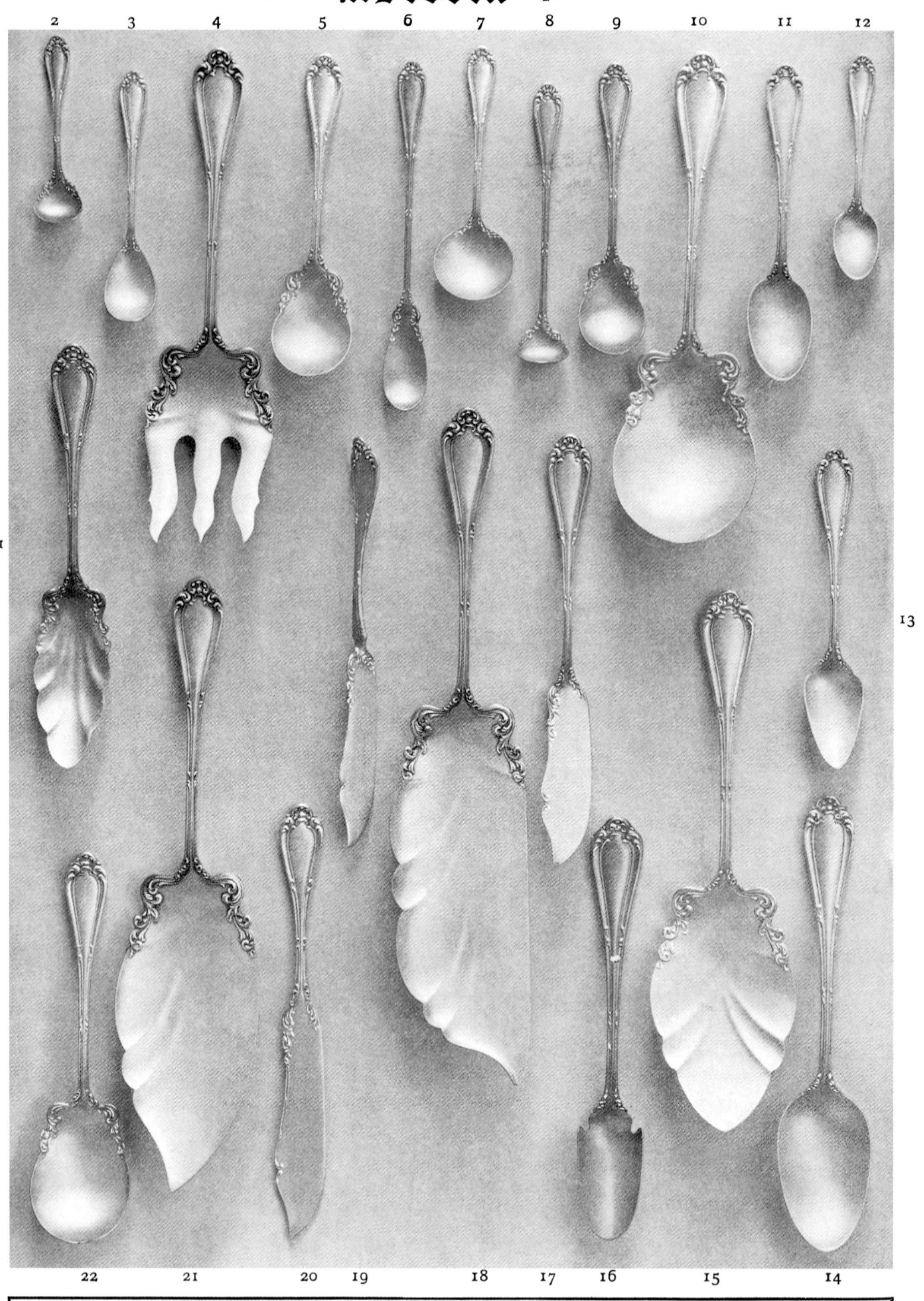

Cuts one-third actual size

1 Jelly Knife	6 Horse-radish Spoon	10 Berry Spoon	15 Pie Knife	19 Butter Knife, twist
2 Salt Spoon	7 Bouillon Spoon	11 Tea Spoon	16 Cheese Scoop	20 Individual Fish Knife
3 Egg Spoon	8 Mustard Spoon	12 Coffee Spoon	17 Butter Knife, spoon handle	21 Fish Knife, serving
4 Fish Fork	9 Ice Cream Spoon	13 Orange Spoon	18 Crumb Knife	22 Jelly Spoon
5 Sugar Shell		14 Dessert Spoon		

Trade Mark
"1835 - R. WALLACE"

The "Astoria" Table Cutlery

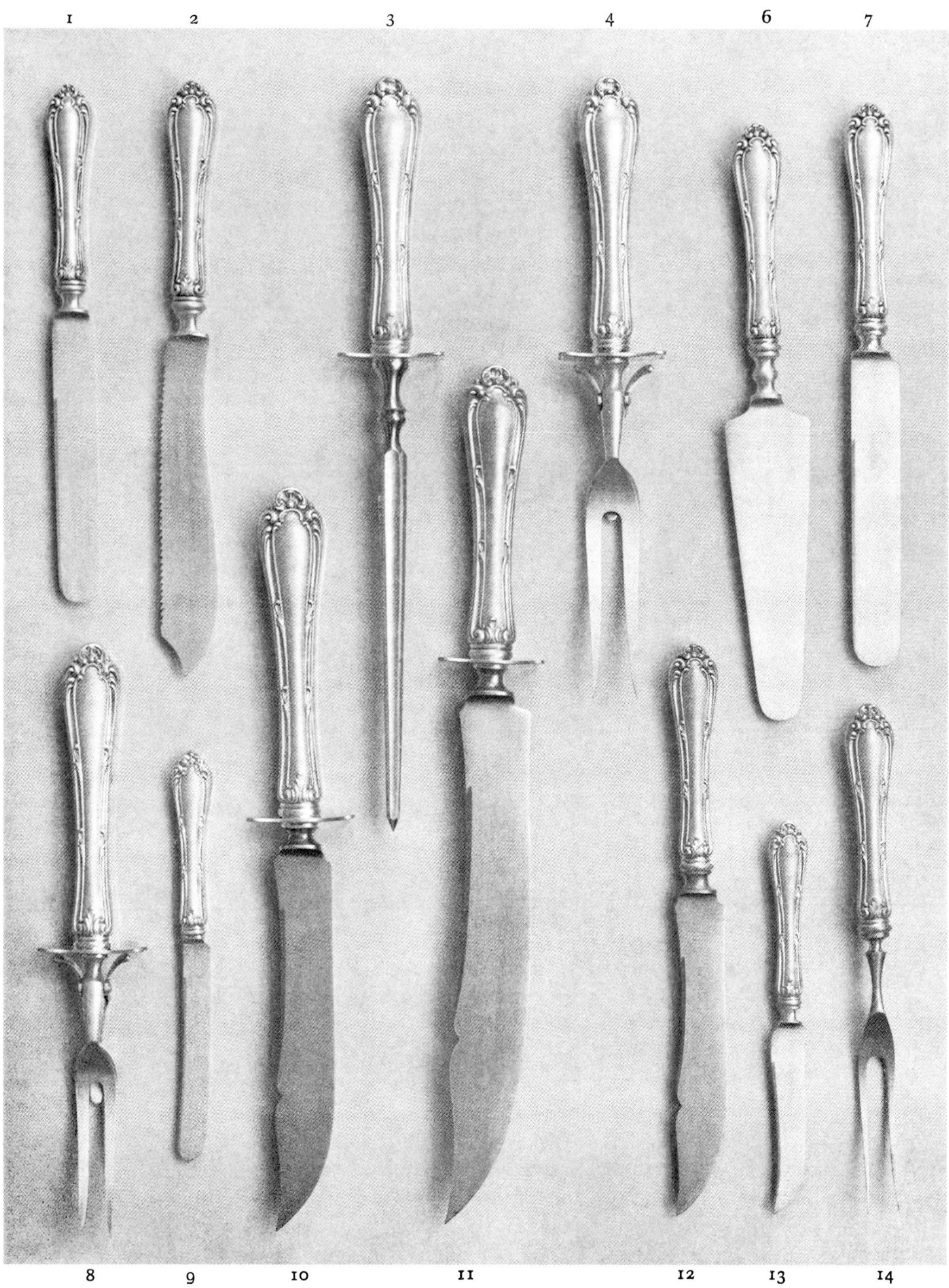

Cuts one-third actual size			
1 Dessert Knife 2 Cake Knife 3 Steel 4 Meat Carving Fork	6 Pie Server 7 Medium Knife 8 Game Carving Fork	9 Orange Knife 10 Game Carving Knife 11 Meat Carving Knife	12 Tête-à-Tête Carving Knife 13 Fruit Knife 14 Tête-à-Tête Fork

36

Trade Mark
"1835–R. WALLACE"

The "Astoria" Pattern

LIST AND PRICES OF ARTICLES MADE IN THE "ASTORIA" PATTERN

		Extra Plate	Sectional Plate	Triple Plate
SPOONS				
Five o'clock Teas	doz.	$4.75	....	$6.50
Tea spoons, large	"	4.75	$5.50	6.50
Dessert spoons	"	8.50	9.50	11.00
Soup spoons	"	9.50	11.00	13.00
Table spoons	"	9.50	11.00	13.00
FORKS				
Dessert forks	doz.	8.50	9.50	11.00
Medium forks	"	9.50	11.00	13.00

		Extra Plate	Triple Plate	Gilding Extra
FORKS				
[1]Asparagus	each	4.00	5.50	1.50
[2]Berry	doz.	6.00	7.50	3.00
[1]Cake	each	1.25	1.75	.50
Child's	"	.60	.85	....
[1]Cold Meat, large	"	1.25	1.75	.50
[1]Cold Meat, small	"	1.05	1.50	.35
[1]Fish, serving	"	3.50	4.15	.75
[2]Fish, individual	doz.	11.00	13.50	4.00
[2]Ice cream	"	7.50	10.00	4.00
[1]Lettuce	each	1.75	2.25	.50
Olive	"	.75	1.00	.35
[2]Oyster	doz.	6.30	7.50	4.00
Pickle, long	each	1.00	1.25	.35
Pickle, short	"	.75	1.00	.35
[2]Pie	doz.	9.50	12.50	4.00
[1]Salad, serving	each	3.50	4.15	.75
[2]Salad, individual	doz.	9.50	12.50	4.00
[1]Sardine	each	1.25	1.50	.35
KNIVES				
[3]Butter, twist	each	.90	1.25	.35
[3] " spoon handle	"	.75	1.10	.35
[2]Butter, individual	doz.	8.50	10.50	4.00
[1]Cake	each	3.50	4.50	.75
Child's	"	.75	1.00	....
[1]Crumb	"	4.00	5.00	1.00
[1]Fish, serving	"	3.50	4.50	1.00
[2]Fish, individual	doz.	12.00	16.00	6.00
[1]Jelly	each	1.50	1.75	.50
[1]Pie	"	2.50	3.50	.75

		Extra Plate	Triple Plate	Gilding Extra
LADLES				
[1]Cream	each	$1.15	$1.65	$ .50
[1]Gravy	"	1.50	2.25	.75
[1]Medium	"	4.00	6.00	1.00
[1]Oyster	"	3.25	4.75	1.00
[1]Punch	"	6.00	....	1.50
[1]Soup	"	4.25	6.25	1.25
[1]Soup, individual	"	2.25	3.50	1.00
SERVERS				
[1]Asparagus	each	4.25	6.25	1.50
[1]Cucumber	"	2.00	2.50	.75
[1]Ice cream	"	3.50	4.50	1.00
SCOOPS				
[1]Cheese, large	each	1.65	2.25	.35
[1]Cheese, small	"	1.50	2.00	.35
SLICERS				
[1]Ice cream	each	3.50	4.50	.75
SPOONS				
[1]Berry	each	2.00	3.00	.75
[2]Bouillon	doz.	9.00	12.00	4.00
Child's	each	.40	.55	....
[2]Coffee	doz.	4.70	6.20	3.00
[2]Egg	"	5.25	7.00	3.00
[1]Horse-radish	each	.75	1.00	.25
[1]Ice	"	2.00	3.00	.75
[2]Ice cream	doz.	5.25	7.00	3.00
Mustard	each	.40	.55	.18
[2]Orange	doz.	6.00	8.50	4.00
[1]Preserve	each	1.60	2.10	.75
[1]Salad, serving	"	2.00	3.00	.75
Salt, large	doz.	4.20	5.50	2.00
Salt, small	"	3.70	5.00	2.00
[3]Sugar	each	.75	1.00	.35
TONGS				
[1]Sugar	each	....	....	....
[1]Tête-à-tête	"	1.50	2.00	.50
[1]CHILD'S SET				
Spoon, fork and flat handle knife	Per set	2.00	2.65	....
With hollow handle knife, steel blade	Per set	2.85	3.45	....
With pearl handle knife, steel blade	Per set	4.25	....	....

[1] Each in satin-lined box [2] Set of six in satin-lined box [3] Satin-lined boxes 15 cents extra

Table Cutlery

HANDLES MADE OF GERMAN SILVER, SILVER SOLDERED—BLADES OF THE HIGHEST QUALITY AND FINEST TEMPERED STEEL, PLATED WITH HEAVY TRIPLE PLATE—IN SATIN-LINED BOXES

KNIVES			KNIVES			CARVING SETS		
[1]Medium	per doz.,	$13.00	[1]Fruit	per doz.,	$11.00	[2]Meat, 3 pieces	per set,	$8.40
[1]Dessert	"	12.00	[1] [2]Orange, saw back	"	12.00	[2]Game, 2 pieces	"	5.00
[1]Cake, saw back,	each,	1.75	[1] [2]Pie Server	each,	1.75	[2]Tête-à-tête, 2 pieces	"	3.50

[1] Plated Blades [2] In Satin-lined boxes

Trade Mark
"1835 – R. WALLACE"

The "Anjou" Pattern

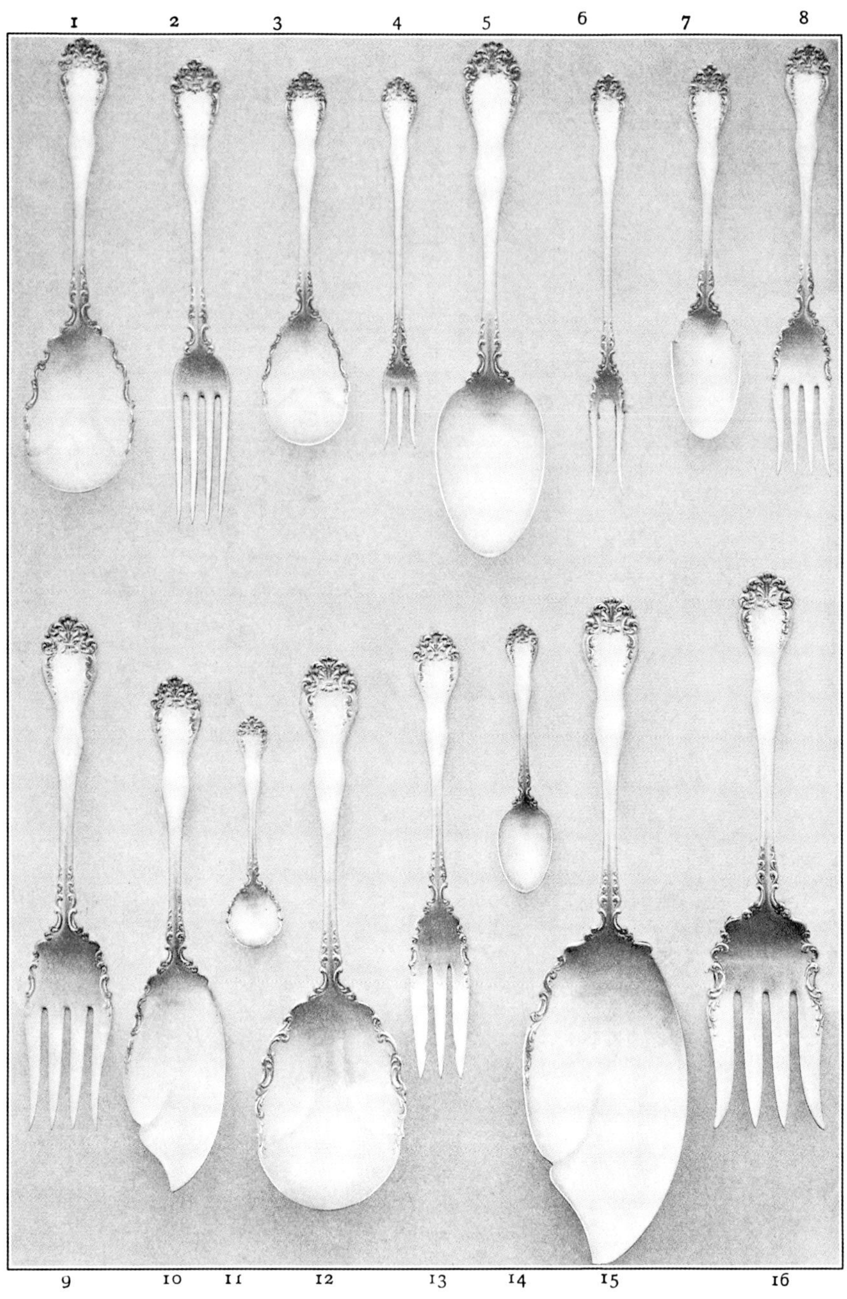

Illustrations one-third size

1 Preserve Spoon	5 Table Spoon	9 Large Cold Meat Fork	13 Pastry Fork
2 Medium Fork	6 Olive Fork	10 Jelly Knife	14 Coffee Spoon
3 Sugar Spoon	7 Small Cheese Scoop	11 Large Salt Spoon	15 Ice Cream Knife
4 Oyster Fork	8 Individual Fish Fork	12 Salad Spoon	16 Salad Fork

38

Trade Mark
"1835 – R. WALLACE"

The "Anjou" pattern

Illustrations one-third size

1 Ice Cream Spoon	5 Sardine Fork	9 Child's Fork	13 Teaspoon
2 Dessert Spoon	6 Dessert Fork	10 Child's Knife	14 Soup Spoon
3 Orange Spoon	7 Ice Cream Fork	11 Child's Spoon	15 Berry Fork
4 Gravy Ladle	8 Fish Knife	12 Berry Spoon	16 Fish Fork

39

Trade Mark
"1835–R. WALLACE"

The "Anjou" Pattern

LIST AND PRICES OF ARTICLES MADE IN THE "ANJOU" PATTERN

		Extra Plate	Sectional Plate	Triple Plate
SPOONS				
Five o'clock Teas	doz.	$4.50	....	$6.50
Tea spoons, large	"	4.75	$5.50	6.50
Dessert spoons	"	8.50	9.50	11.00
Soup spoons	"	9.50	11.00	13.00
Table spoons	"	9.50	11.00	13.00
FORKS				
Dessert forks	doz.	8.50	9.50	11.00
Medium forks	"	9.50	11.00	13.00

		Extra Plate	Triple Plate	Gilding Extra
FORKS				
[1]Asparagus	each	4.00	5.50	1.50
[2]Berry	doz.	6.00	7.50	3.00
[1]Cake	each	1.25	1.75	.50
Child's	"	.60	.85	....
[1]Cold Meat, large	"	1.25	1.75	.50
[1]Cold Meat, small	"	1.05	1.50	.35
[1]Fish, serving	"	3.50	4.15	.75
[2]Fish, individual	doz.	11.00	13.50	4.00
[2]Ice Cream	"	7.50	10.00	4.00
[1]Lettuce	each	1.75	2.25	.50
Olive	"	.75	1.00	.35
[2]Oyster	doz.	6.30	7.50	4.00
Pickle, long	each	1.00	1.25	.35
Pickle, short	"	.75	1.00	.35
[2]Pie	doz.	9.50	12.50	4.00
[1]Salad, serving	each	3.50	4.15	.75
[2]Salad, individual	doz.	9.50	12.50	4.00
[1]Sardine	each	1.25	1.50	.35
KNIVES				
[3]Butter, twist	each	.90	1.25	.35
[3] " spoon handle	"	.75	1.10	.35
[2] " individual	doz.	8.50	10.50	4.00
Child's	each	.75	1.00	....
[1]Crumb	"	4.00	5.00	1.00
[1]Fish, serving	"	3.50	4.50	1.00
[2]Fish, individual	doz.	12.00	16.00	6.00
[1]Jelly	each	1.50	1.75	.50
[1]Pie	"	2.50	3.50	.75

		Extra Plate	Triple Plate	Gilding Extra
LADLES				
[1]Cream	each	$1.15	$1.65	$ .50
[1]Gravy	"	1.50	2.25	.75
[1]Medium	"	4.00	6.00	1.00
[1]Oyster	"	3.25	4.75	1.00
[1]Punch	"	6.00	....	1.50
[1]Soup	"	4.25	6.25	1.25
[1]Soup, individual	"	2.25	3.50	1.00
PICKS				
Nut Picks	doz.	4.00	5.00	....
SERVERS				
[1]Asparagus	each	4.25	6.25	1.50
[1]Cucumber	"	2.00	2.50	.75
[1]Ice Cream	"	3.50	4.50	1.00
SCOOPS				
[1]Cheese, large	each	1.65	2.25	.35
[1]Cheese, small	"	1.50	2.00	.35
SLICERS				
[1]Ice Cream	each	3.50	4.50	.75
SPOONS				
[1]Berry	each	2.00	3.00	.75
[1]Bouillon	doz.	9.00	12.00	4.00
Child's	each	.40	.55	....
[2]Coffee	doz.	4.70	6.20	3.00
[2]Egg	"	5.25	7.00	3.00
[1]Ice	each	2.00	3.00	.75
[2]Ice Cream	doz.	5.25	7.00	3.00
[1]Individual salt	"	3.70	5.00	2.00
Mustard	each	.40	.55	.18
[2]Orange	doz.	6.00	8.50	4.00
[1]Preserve	each	1.60	2.10	.75
[1]Salad, serving	"	2.00	3.00	.75
Salt, large	doz.	4.20	5.50	2.00
[3]Sugar	each	.75	1.00	.35
TONGS				
[1]Sugar	each	1.50	2.00	.50
[1]Ice	doz.	46.00	64.00	....
[1]Asparagus	"	50.00	68.00	....
[1]CHILD'S SET				
Spoon, fork and flat handle knife	Per set	2.00	2.65	....
With hollow handle knife, steel blade	Per set	2.85	3.45	....
With pearl handle knife, steel blade	Per set	4.25	....	....

[1] Each in satin-lined box   [2] Set of six in satin-lined box   [3] Satin-lined boxes 15 cents extra

Table Cutlery

HANDLES MADE OF GERMAN SILVER, SILVER SOLDERED—BLADES OF THE HIGHEST QUALITY AND FINEST TEMPERED STEEL, PLATED WITH HEAVY TRIPLE PLATE—IN SATIN-LINED BOXES

KNIVES

[1]Medium	per doz.,	$13.00
[1]Dessert	"	12.00
[1]Cake, saw back,	each,	1.75

KNIVES

[1]Fruit	per doz.,	$11.00
[1] [2]Orange, saw back	"	12.00
[1] [2]Pie Server	each,	1.75

CARVING SETS

[2]Meat, 3 pieces	per set,	$8.40
[2]Game, 2 pieces	"	5.00
[2]Tête-à-tête, 2 pieces	"	3.50

[1] Plated Blades   [2] In satin-lined boxes

The "Joan" Pattern

Cuts one-third actual size			For price list see next page
1 Smoked Beef Fork 2 Cucumber Server 3 Pie Fork 4 Pickle Fork	5 Punch Ladle 6 Lettuce Fork 7 Ice Cream Fork 8 Soup Spoon, round bowl	9 Sardine Fork 10 Cake Knife 11 Tea Spoon 12 Cold Meat Fork	13 Medium Fork 14 Dessert Fork 15 Medium Knife

Trade Mark
"1835 – R. WALLACE"

The "Joan" Pattern

LIST AND PRICES OF ARTICLES MADE IN THE "JOAN" PATTERN

		Extra Plate	Sectional Plate	Triple Plate
SPOONS				
Five o'clock Teas	doz.	$4.75	....	$6.50
Tea spoons, large	"	4.75	$5.50	6.50
Dessert spoons	"	8.50	9.50	11.00
Soup spoons	"	9.50	11.00	13.00
Table spoons	"	9.50	11.00	13.00
FORKS				
Dessert forks	doz.	8.50	9.50	11.00
Medium forks	"	9.50	11.00	13.00

		Extra Plate	Triple Plate	Gilding Extra
FORKS				
[1]Asparagus	each	4.00	5.50	1.50
[2]Berry	doz.	6.00	7.50	3.00
[1]Cake	each	1.25	1.75	.50
Child's	"	.60	.85	....
[1]Cold Meat, large	"	1.25	1.75	.50
[1]Cold Meat, small	"	1.05	1.50	.35
[1]Fish, serving	"	3.50	4.15	.75
[2]Fish, individual	doz.	11.00	13.50	4.00
[2]Ice cream	"	7.50	10.00	4.00
[1]Lettuce	each	1.75	2.25	.50
Olive	"	.75	1.00	.35
[2]Oyster	doz.	6.30	7.50	4.00
Pickle, long	each	1.00	1.25	.35
Pickle, short	"	.75	1.00	.35
[2]Pie	doz.	9.50	12.50	4.00
[1]Salad, serving	each	3.50	4.15	.75
[2]Salad, individual	doz.	9.50	12.50	4.00
[1]Sardine	each	1.25	1.50	.35
KNIVES				
[3]Butter, twist	each	.90	1.25	.35
[3] " spoon handle	"	.75	1.10	.35
[2]Butter, individual	doz.	8.50	10.50	4.00
[1]Cake	each	3.50	4.50	.75
Child's	"	.75	1.00	....
[1]Crumb	"	4.00	5.00	1.00
[1]Fish, serving	"	3.50	4.50	1.00
[2]Fish, individual	doz.	12.00	16.00	6.00
[1]Jelly	each	1.50	1.75	.50
[1]Pie	"	2.50	3.50	.75

		Extra Plate	Triple Plate	Gilding Extra
LADLES				
[1]Cream	each	$1.15	$1.65	$ .50
[1]Gravy	"	1.50	2.25	.75
[1]Medium	"	4.00	6.00	1.00
[1]Oyster	"	3.25	4.75	1.00
[1]Punch	"	6.00	....	1.50
[1]Soup	"	4.25	6.25	1.25
[1]Soup, individual	"	2.25	3.50	1.00
SERVERS				
[1]Asparagus	each	4.25	6.25	1.50
[1]Cucumber	"	2.00	2.50	.75
[1]Ice cream	"	3.50	4.50	1.00
SCOOPS				
[1]Cheese, large	each	1.65	2.25	.35
[1]Cheese, small	"	1.50	2.00	.35
SLICERS				
[1]Ice cream	each	3.50	4.50	.75
SPOONS				
[1]Berry	each	2.00	3.00	.75
[2]Bouillon	doz.	9.00	12.00	4.00
Child's	each	.40	.55	....
[2]Coffee	doz.	4.70	6.20	3.00
[2]Egg	"	5.25	7.00	3.00
[1]Horse-radish	each	.75	1.00	.25
[1]Ice	"	2.00	3.00	.75
[2]Ice cream	doz.	5.25	7.00	3.00
Mustard	each	.40	.55	.18
[2]Orange	doz.	6.00	8.50	4.00
[1]Preserve	each	1.60	2.10	.75
[1]Salad, serving	"	2.00	3.00	.75
Salt, large	doz.	4.20	5.50	2.00
Salt, small	"	3.70	5.00	2.00
[3]Sugar	each	.75	1.00	.35
TONGS				
[1]Sugar	each	....	....	....
[1]Tête-à-tête	"	1.50	2.00	.50
[1]CHILD'S SET				
Spoon, fork and flat handle knife	Per set	2.00	2.65	....
With hollow handle knife, steel blade	Per set	2.85	3.45	....
With pearl handle knife, steel blade	Per set	4.25	....	....

[1] Each in satin-lined box [2] Set of six in satin-lined box [3] Satin-lined boxes 15 cents extra

		Extra Plate	Triple Plate
Nut Pick	per doz.	$4.00	$5.00
Cracker Scoop	" "	28.00	40.00
Julip Strainer	" "	13.00	19.00
Asparagus Tongs	per doz.	$50.00	$68.00
Ice Tongs	" "	46.00	64.00

[1] Each in satin-lined box [2] Set of six in satin-lined box [3] Satin-lined boxes 15 cents extra

Trade Mark
"1835 - R. WALLACE"

The "Stuart" Pattern

Illustrations one-third size

1 Child's Spoon 2 Soup Spoon 3 Coffee Spoon 4 Table Spoon 5 Dessert Spoon	6 Tea Spoon 7 Bouillon Spoon 8 Ice Cream Fork 9 Child's Fork 10 Dessert Fork	11 Cold Meat Fork 12 Medium Fork 13 Butter Knife 14 Oyster Fork

43

Trade Mark
"1835 – R. WALLACE"

The "Stuart" pattern

Illustrations one-third size

1 Egg Spoon 2 Ice Cream Spoon 3 Sugar Spoon 4 Berry Spoon	5 Preserve Spoon 6 Orange Spoon 7 Pie Knife 8 Jelly Knife	9 Child's Knife 10 Tomato Server 11 Cheese Scoop, large

44

Trade Mark
"1835 – R. WALLACE"

The "Stuart" Pattern

SOLID-HANDLE KNIVES and FORKS

Warranted 12 dwt. Plate.

THESE knives are made of the best crucible steel, and are plated in the following manner:—

They first receive a coating of Copper; they are then heavily plated with Nickel, and afterward with Pure Silver. Nickel-plate not only doubles the durability of the goods, but, being nearly impervious to moisture, renders knives so plated much less liable to rust than those plated in the ordinary way.

The forks are made of German or Nickel-silver, and are plated with an extra heavy plate of silver, equal to that on the knives.

PRICES

Table Knives . . . . . . per doz.	$10.50
Table Forks	10.50
Dessert Knives	9.50
Dessert Forks	9.50

Table Knife

Illustrations Full Size

Table Fork

Trade Mark
"1835 – R. Wallace"

The "Stuart" Pattern

LIST AND PRICES OF ARTICLES MADE IN THE "STUART" PATTERN

		Extra Plate	Sectional Plate	Triple Plate
SPOONS				
Five o'clock Teas	doz.	$4.75	....	$6.50
Tea spoons, large	"	4.75	$5.50	6.50
Dessert spoons	"	8.50	9.50	11.00
Soup spoons	"	9.50	11.00	13.00
Table spoons	"	9.50	11.00	13.00
FORKS				
Dessert forks	doz.	8.50	9.50	11.00
Medium forks	"	9.50	11.00	13.00

		Extra Plate	Triple Plate	Gilding Extra
FORKS				
[1]Asparagus	each	4.00	5.50	1.50
[2]Berry	doz.	6.00	7.50	3.00
[1]Cake	each	1.25	1.75	.50
Child's	"	.60	.85	....
[1]Cold Meat, large	"	1.25	1.75	.50
[1]Cold Meat, small	"	1.05	1.50	.35
[1]Fish, serving	"	3.50	4.15	.75
[2]Fish, individual	doz.	11.00	13.50	4.00
[2]Ice cream	"	7.50	10.00	4.00
[1]Lettuce	each	1.75	2.25	.50
Olive	"	.75	1.00	.35
[2]Oyster	doz.	6.30	7.50	4.00
Pickle, long	each	1.00	1.25	.35
Pickle, short	"	.75	1.00	.35
[2]Pie	doz.	9.50	12.50	4.00
[1]Salad, serving	each	3.50	4.15	.75
[2]Salad, individual	doz.	9.50	12.50	4.00
[1]Sardine	each	1.25	1.50	.35
KNIVES				
[3]Butter, twist	each	.90	1.25	.35
[3] " spoon handle	"	.75	1.10	.35
[2]Butter, individual	doz.	8.50	10.50	4.00
[1]Cake	each	3.50	4.50	.75
Child's	"	.75	1.00	....
[1]Crumb	"	4.00	5.00	1.00
[1]Fish, serving	"	3.50	4.50	1.00
[2]Fish, individual	doz.	12.00	16.00	6.00
[1]Jelly	each	1.50	1.75	.50
[1]Pie	"	2.50	3.50	.75

		Extra Plate	Triple Plate	Gilding Extra
LADLES				
[1]Cream	each	$1.15	$1.65	$ .50
[1]Gravy	"	1.50	2.25	.75
[1]Medium	"	4.00	6.00	1.00
[1]Oyster	"	3.25	4.75	1.00
[1]Punch	"	6.00	....	1.50
[1]Soup	"	4.25	6.25	1.25
[1]Soup, individual	"	2.25	3.50	1.00
SERVERS				
[1]Asparagus	each	4.25	6.25	1.50
[1]Cucumber	"	2.00	2.50	.75
[1]Ice Cream	"	3.50	4.50	1.00
SCOOPS				
[1]Cheese, large	each	1.65	2.25	.35
[1]Cheese, small	"	1.50	2.00	.35
SLICERS				
[1]Ice cream	each	3.50	4.50	.75
SPOONS				
[1]Berry	each	2.00	3.00	.75
[2]Bouillon	doz.	9.00	12.00	4.00
Child's	each	.40	.55	....
[2]Coffee	doz.	4.70	6.20	3.00
[2]Egg	"	5.25	7.00	3.00
[1]Ice	each	2.00	3.00	.75
[2]Ice cream	doz.	5.25	7.00	3.00
Mustard	each	.40	.55	.18
[2]Orange	doz.	6.00	8.50	4.00
[1]Preserve	each	1.60	2.10	.75
[1]Salad, serving	"	2.00	3.00	.75
Salt, large	doz.	4.20	5.50	2.00
[3]Sugar	each	.75	1.00	.35
TONGS				
[1]Sugar	each	....	....	....
[1]Tête-à-tête	"	1.50	2.00	.50
[1]CHILD'S SET				
Spoon, fork and flat handle knife	Per set	2.00	2.65	....
With hollow handle knife, steel blade	Per set	2.85	3.45	....
With pearl handle knife, steel blade	Per set	4.25	....	....

[1] Each in satin-lined box [2] Set of six in satin-lined box [3] Satin-lined boxes 15 cents extra

Table Cutlery

HANDLES MADE OF GERMAN SILVER, SILVER SOLDERED—BLADES OF THE HIGHEST QUALITY AND FINEST TEMPERED STEEL, PLATED WITH HEAVY TRIPLE PLATE—IN SATIN-LINED BOXES

KNIVES			KNIVES			CARVING SETS		
[1]Medium	per doz.,	$13.00	[1]Fruit	per doz.,	$11.00	[2]Meat, 3 pieces	per set,	$8.40
[1]Dessert	"	12.00	[1][2]Orange, saw back	"	12.00	[2]Game, 2 pieces	"	5.00
[1]Cake, saw back,	each,	1.75	[1][2]Pie Server	each,	1.75	[2]Tête-à-tête, 2 pieces	"	3.50

[1] Plated Blades [2] In Satin-lined boxes

Trade Mark
"1835-R. WALLACE"

No. 7700

No. 7400

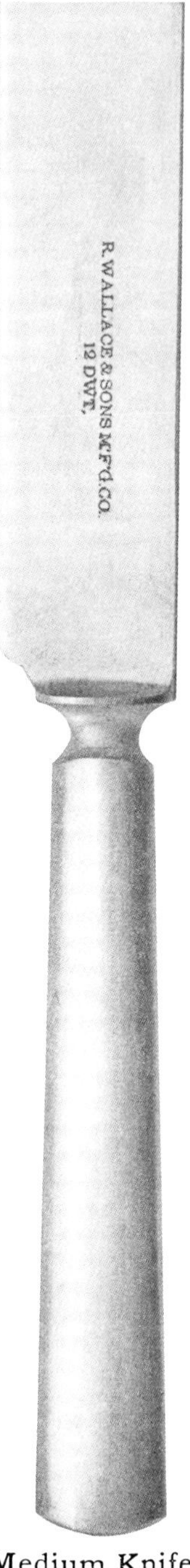

Solid Steel

Warranted 12 dwt. Plate.

These knives first receive a coating of Copper; they are then heavily plated with Nickel, and afterward with Pure Silver. Nickel-plate not only doubles the durability of the goods, but, being nearly impervious to moisture, renders knives so plated much less liable to rust than those plated in the ordinary way.

PRICE

Table Knives	. per doz.,	$10.00
Dessert "	. per doz.,	9.00

Medium Knife

Handles Full Size

Medium Knife

The "Floral" Pattern

Trade Mark
"1835-R. WALLACE"

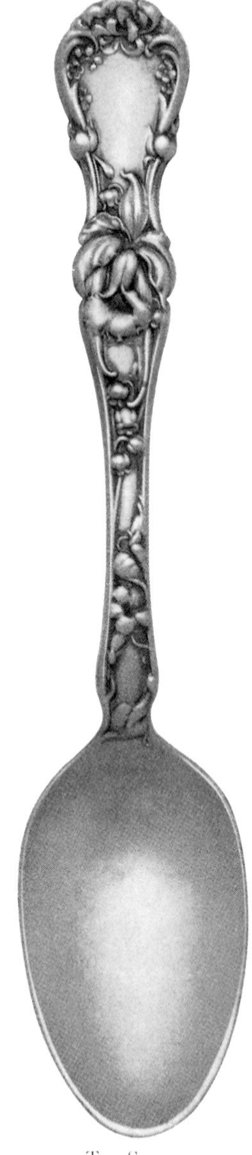

Tea Spoon
Full Size

THIS new service, perhaps more than the others, most forcibly convinces one of the superiority of the "1835-R. Wallace" silver plate in all vital points.

Look at the illustrations of the Tea Spoon. Did you ever see such graceful designing and beautiful die cutting in a plated spoon before, or the back of a handle brought up to such a state of perfection?

There is no plated ware made that will approach this pattern in exquisite workmanship and finish.

With the exception of the fancy pieces, the "Floral Pattern" is carried in triple plate only, and the entire service is finished exclusively in French Gray.

R. WALLACE & SONS MFG. CO.

Wallingford, Conn.

NEW YORK
CHICAGO

SAN FRANCISCO
LONDON

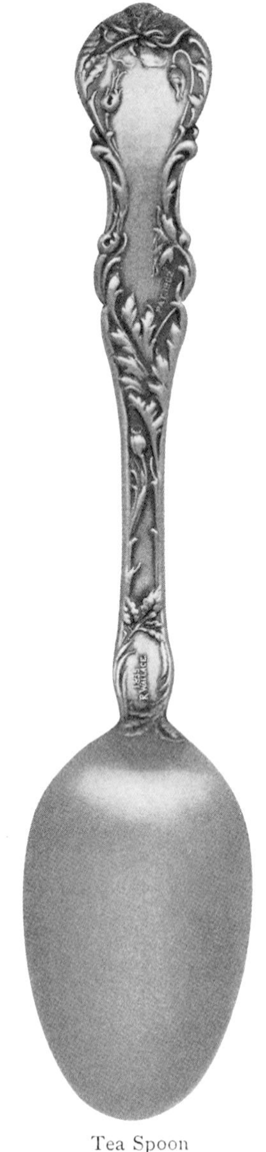

Tea Spoon
Reverse
Full Size

Trade Mark
"1835–R. WALLACE"

The "Floral" Pattern

Illustrations one-third size

1 Soup Spoon
2 Table Spoon
3 Soup Ladle
4 Gravy Ladle
5 Dessert Spoon
6 Cream Ladle
7 Bouillon Spoon
8 Pie Knife
9 Coffee Spoon
10 Berry Spoon
11 Sugar Spoon
12 Child's Spoon

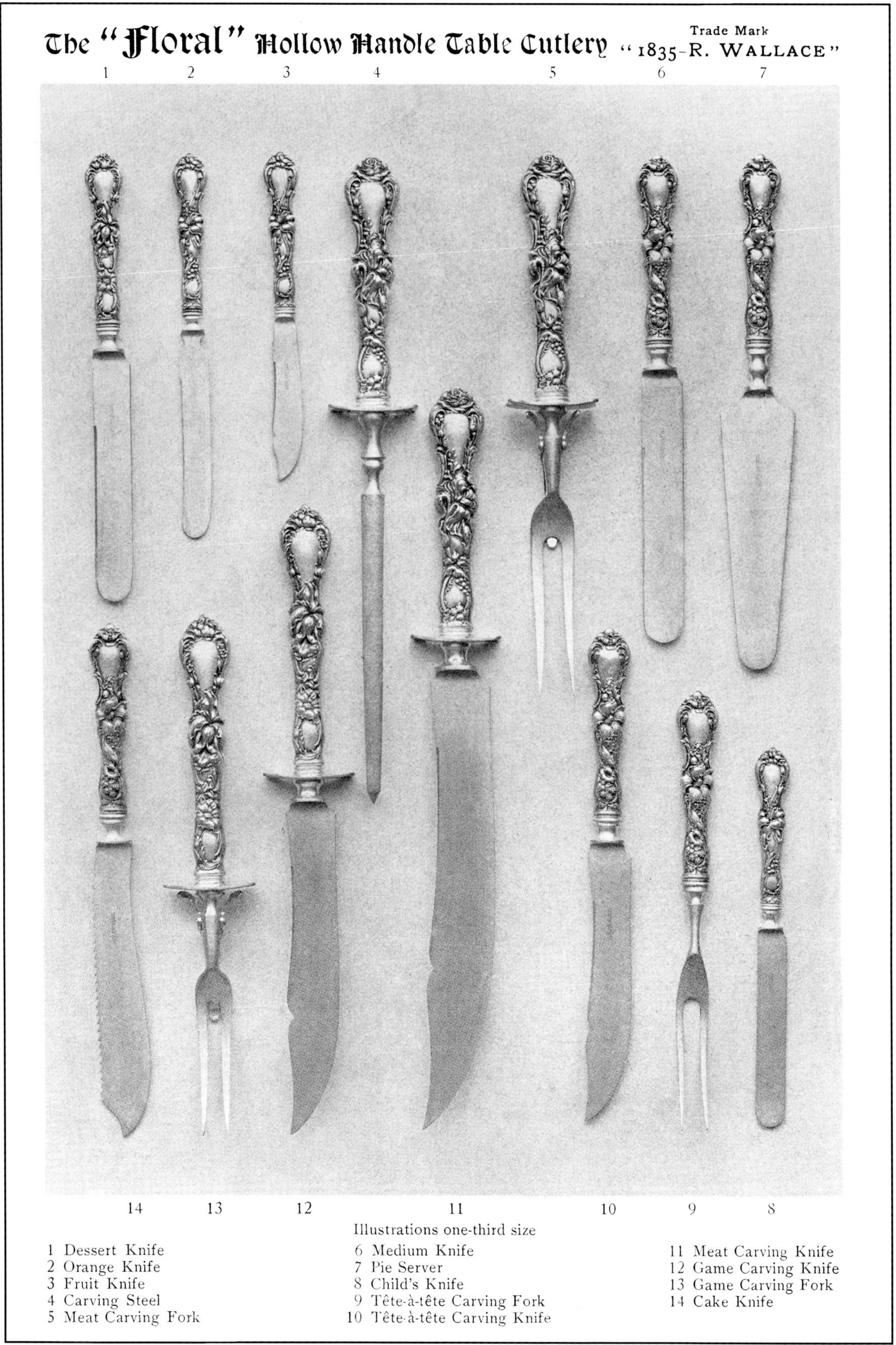

The "Floral" Hollow Handle Table Cutlery

Trade Mark "1835-R. WALLACE"

1 2 3 4 5 6 7

14 13 12 11 10 9 8

Illustrations one-third size

1 Dessert Knife
2 Orange Knife
3 Fruit Knife
4 Carving Steel
5 Meat Carving Fork
6 Medium Knife
7 Pie Server
8 Child's Knife
9 Tête-à-tête Carving Fork
10 Tête-à-tête Carving Knife
11 Meat Carving Knife
12 Game Carving Knife
13 Game Carving Fork
14 Cake Knife

Trade Mark
"1835-R. WALLACE" **The "Floral" Pattern**

LIST AND PRICES OF ARTICLES MADE IN THE "FLORAL" PATTERN

		Triple Plate
SPOONS		
Five o'clock Teas	per doz.	$6.50
Tea spoons, large	,,	6.50
Dessert spoons	,,	11.00
Soup spoons	,,	13.00
Table spoons	,,	13.00
FORKS		
Dessert forks	per doz.	11.00
Medium forks	,,	13.00

		Extra Plate	Triple Plate	Gilding Extra
FORKS				
[1]Asparagus	per doz.	$48.00	$66.00	$18.00
[2]Berry	,,	6.00	7.50	3.00
[1]Cake	,,	15.00	21.00	6.00
Child's	,,	7.00	10.00	....
[1]Cold Meat, large	,,	15.00	21.00	6.00
[1]Cold Meat, small	,,	12.50	18.00	4.00
[1]Fish, serving	,,	42.00	50.00	9.00
[2]Fish, individual	,,	11.00	13.50	4.00
[2]Ice Cream	,,	7.50	10.00	4.00
[1]Lettuce	,,	20.00	27.00	6.00
[3]Olive	,,	9.00	12.00	4.00
[2]Oyster	,,	6.30	7.50	4.00
[3]Pickle	,,	12.00	15.00	4.00
Pie	,,	9.50	12.50	4.00
[1]Salad, serving	,,	42.00	50.00	9.00
[2]Salad, individual	,,	9.50	12.50	4.00
[1]Sardine	,,	15.00	18.00	4.00
KNIVES				
[3]Butter, twist	per doz.	10.50	14.50	4.00
[3] ,, spoon handle	,,	10.50	14.50	4.00
[2] ,, spreader	,,	8.50	10.50	4.00
Child's	,,	9.00	12.00	....
[1]Crumb	,,	48.00	60.00	12.00
[1]Fish, serving	,,	42.00	54.00	12.00
[2]Fish, individual	,,	12.00	16.00	6.00
[1]Pie	,,	30.00	42.00	9.00

		Extra Plate	Triple Plate	Gilding Extra
LADLES				
[1]Cream	per doz.	$15.00	$21.00	$6.00
[1]Gravy	,,	21.00	30.00	9.00
[1]Medium	,,	50.00	74.00	12.00
[1]Oyster	,,	42.00	60.00	10.00
[1]Punch	,,	72.00	....	18.00
[1]Soup	,,	54.00	78.00	15.00
PICKS				
Nut	per doz.	4.00	5.00	....
SERVERS				
[1]Asparagus	per doz.	51.00	75.00	18.00
[1]Cucumber, small	,,	16.00	19.00	6.00
[1]Ice Cream	,,	42.00	54.00	12.00
[1]Tomato	,,	24.00	30.00	9.00
SCOOPS				
[1]Cheese, large	per doz.	20.00	27.00	4.00
[1]Cheese, small	,,	18.00	24.00	4.00
SPOONS				
[1]Berry	per doz.	24.00	36.00	9.00
[2]Bouillon	,,	9.00	12.00	4.00
Child's	,,	....	6.50	....
Chocolate	,,	5.50	7.25	3.00
Chocolate Muddler	,,	10.20	14.40	4.00
[1]Jelly	,,	18.00	24.00	6.00
[3]Pap	,,	9.00	11.00	4.00
[1]Platter	,,	30.00	42.00	....
[2]Coffee	,,	4.70	6.20	3.00
[2]Egg	,,	5.25	7.00	3.00
[1]Ice	,,	24.00	36.00	9.00
[2]Ice Cream	,,	6.25	8.00	3.00
Mustard	,,	4.70	6.40	2.00
[2]Orange	,,	6.00	8.50	4.00
[1]Preserve	,,	19.00	25.00	6.00
[1]Salad, serving	,,	24.00	36.00	9.00
Salt, large	,,	4.20	5.50	2.00
[3]Sugar	,,	9.00	11.00	4.00
TONGS				
[1]Sugar	per doz.	18.00	24.00	6.00
Ice	,,	46.00	64.00	....
[1]CHILD'S SET				
Spoon, fork and flat handle knife	Per doz. sets.	24.00	31.50	....
With hollow handle knife, steel blade	Per doz. sets.	34.00	41.50	....
With pearl handle knife, steel blade	Per doz. sets.	52.00	59.50	....

[1] Each in satin-lined box [2] Set of six in satin-lined box [3] Satin-lined boxes, $2.00 per doz. extra

Table Cutlery

HANDLES MADE OF GERMAN SILVER, SILVER SOLDERED—BLADES OF THE HIGHEST QUALITY AND FINEST TEMPERED STEEL, PLATED WITH HEAVY PLATE—IN SATIN-LINED BOXES
MEDIUM AND DESSERT KNIVES ARE PLATED WITH 16 DWT. PLATE ONLY

KNIVES

[1]Medium	per doz.,	$15.00
[1]Dessert	,,	14.00
[1]Cake, saw back,	,,	21.00

KNIVES

[1]Fruit	per doz.,	$11.00
[1] [2]Orange, saw back	,,	12.00
[1] [2]Pie Server	,,	21.00
[1]Child's Knife	,,	11.50

CARVING SETS

[2]Meat, 3 pieces,	per set,	$8.40
[2]Game, 2 pieces,	,,	5.00
[2]Tête-à-tête, 2 pieces,	,,	3.50

[1] Plated blades [2] In satin-lined boxes